GROW WHAT
YOU LOVE

A Firefly Book

Published by Firefly Books Ltd. 2018
Copyright © 2018 Firefly Books Ltd.
Text copyright © 2018 Emily Murphy
Photographs copyright © as listed on this page
Illustrations copyright © as listed on this page

First printing

Library of Congress Control Number: 2017955586

Library and Archives Canada Cataloguing in Publication
Murphy, Emily, 1969–, author
Grow what you love : 12 food plant families to change your life / by Emily Murphy. Includes bibliographical references and index.
ISBN 978-0-228-10020-1 (softcover)
1. Vegetable gardening. 2. Vegetables. 3. Plants, Edible.
4. Fruit. 5. Herbs. I. Title.
SB321.M87 2018   635   C2017-906483-5

Published in the United States by
Firefly Books (U.S.) Inc.
P.O. Box 1338, Ellicott Station
Buffalo, New York 14205

Published in Canada by
Firefly Books Ltd.
50 Staples Avenue, Unit 1
Richmond Hill, Ontario L4B 0A7

Cover design: Deborah Berne
Back cover and interior design: Marijke Friesen
Editor: Sydney Loney

Printed in China

Unless otherwise specified, all photographs are © Emily Murphy/Josh Murphy.

Photographs © West Cliff Creative: 1, 7, 8, 11, 12, 13, 14, 18, 19, 24–25, 28, 31, 32, 33, 34, 35, 36, 38, 40, 41, 42, 43, 58, 68, 71, 72, 79, 82, 85, 100–101, 118, 119, 140, 142, 143, 162, 168, 176, 178, 183, 190, 194, 200, 202–203, 204, 209, 210, 213, 219, 222, 223, 226, 227, 228, 229, 231, 234, 236, 237, 238, 242, 244, 245, 249, 255, 261, 267, 268; Front Cover (TL & TR), Back Cover (TR), Back Flap.

Unless otherwise specified, all illustrations are © Clover Robin

264: Map courtesy of USDA Agricultural Research Service. Mapping by PRISM Climate Group, Oregon State University, 2012.

265: © Her Majesty the Queen in Right of Canada, as represented by the Minister of Natural Resources Canada, 2014.

GROW
WHAT YOU
LOVE

12 FOOD PLANT FAMILIES TO CHANGE YOUR LIFE

EMILY MURPHY

Firefly Books

CONTENTS

THE SIMPLE ACT OF GROWING

INTRODUCTION

Sometimes the smallest things take up
the most room in your heart

— A. A. MILNE

FINDING JOY IN THE SIMPLE THINGS

When you take time to grow what you love, wonderful things happen. A remarkable yet simple sequence of events unfolds. The small step of planting and growing a handful of beloved ingredients is really **a small step toward approaching life a little differently**, a little more deliberately — and finding beauty in food, nature, seasons and healthy, hand-made living.

When you plant a little, dig a little and harvest often, you discover a process that allows you to live more simply, while adding flavors to meals that can only be found when homegrown. And it all begins by growing what you love. When I began teaching organic gardening, I was surprised by the enthusiasm people took home with them after a class filled with planting, picking and eating. The reaction was overwhelmingly consistent: "If I'd known it was this simple, I would have begun gardening a long time ago!"

It doesn't take much. When friends stop by and a quick hello turns into dinner, panic at an empty fridge subsides when I venture out to the garden and discover an entire wine box overflowing with arugula, waiting to be picked. The result is a simple meal: a pasta dish paired with pesto and fresh arugula salad. (It's a dinner my friends still talk about to this day.)

Grow What You Love is more than a book about gardening and food-making. **It's about cultivating joy and growing all parts of your life:** yourself, your health, time spent with family and nature. It's a lifestyle. When you start planting, you'll discover that your garden, however small, is your nearest touchpoint with nature. It draws you in, just as it draws in birds and butterflies, and is a place of solace and experimentation.

It was many years ago, when I was still a child, that I first fell in love with growing and food-making. My grandmother was my first true guide. Her parents emigrated from Italy and homesteaded on land deep in the Sonoma hills. It was a wild place, with homes speckling the hillsides, but they carved out a simple living

with a large garden and grapes for making wine. I spent my summers there, learning how to find the best berries for cooking, when apples were ripe for picking, and that by growing a few simple ingredients we could make something amazing.

Later, when I went off to college to study botany, I discovered the science behind what I'd learned. Plant physiology, soil science, ecology and taxonomy classes helped me see the building blocks of my childhood with fresh eyes. I became a teacher, studied and practiced garden design, and found myself teaching organic gardening. That's when this book was born — when I asked myself, what am I really trying to say? What is truly important in this life? It came back to love and growing. To me, *Grow What You Love* is a love story disguised as a book about growing and food-making.

WHERE DO YOU BEGIN?

What you need to know to begin growing what you love is all here: the flavors, fragrances, foods and ingredients. *Grow What You Love* is a simple guide to growing a dozen seasonal ingredients that will change the way you cook and live. **It begins with planning your garden and exploring how best to choose plants and recipes you love**, then follows simple methods for garden-to-table growing and seasonal approaches to cooking.

You don't need to grow everything under the sun to make a difference in your life. Instead, focus on the plants that provide abundance with less space and time. Why grow a cabbage that can take half a year to mature when you can grow a seemingly endless supply of leafy greens and sugar snap peas? If it's space that's a constraint, look to plants that grow up rather than out, climbing their way from seed to fruit, and to those packed with the most flavor, like fresh herbs.

In this book, plants are organized by category: tender herbs, summer salads and root vegetables are just a few. Choose a couple to begin with, or maybe one from each group, and grow with a recipe in mind. Once you find success, try a few of the others that challenge your growing skills and stretch your culinary boundaries. The recipes keep the food you've grown front and center and are method-based so you can easily mix and match. Soon, you'll unearth new ways to combine flavors. **The result is garden-fresh bounty worth the effort — and worthy of sharing.**

*Just living is not enough ... one must have
sunshine, freedom and a little flower.*
— HANS CHRISTIAN ANDERSEN

GETTING
STARTED

SET YOUR GARDEN FREE

It's no secret that plants require space to grow, or that sun, soil, water and air are key to a thriving garden. It's the mix that's the mystery — at least at first. How much of each will you need and where will you plant? Figuring this out is your first order of business.

PLANNING YOUR GARDEN

I believe that if you have a container that holds soil and allows for drainage, you've got yourself a garden. A mint tin, an old washtub, a basket, a trash can or a wine box can all be transformed into homes for plants — just add drain holes to the sides and bottom and fill it with soil.

Now, where will your garden live? Do you have a flood of south-facing light coming in through your windows? Or an entryway with plenty of sun and room for both a path and plantings? Rooftops, patios, decks and balconies are also great places to begin. Use walls, fences and hanging gardens to optimize finite space. If your home has limited access to the outdoors, you may find a community garden or sharing the yard of a neighbor your best bet. Setting up an indoor garden with supplemental light is also an option.

My advice for any garden is to start small and grow what you love. Growing in a smaller space makes it manageable; you can build it into your busy schedule and learn as you grow. And by starting with the plants you enjoy cooking with, or simply love looking at, you'll quickly transform the mundane into magic. In fact, this is where the magic begins!

WHERE TO START

- **Start small.** Raised beds, troughs and potted stairway gardens help focus your attention and manage time. You can easily see when to weed and what needs to be watered.

- **Grow what you love.** Find the things that make you happy and grow them, using the plants in the directory to help narrow your choices and find the best varieties for your climate.

☙ **Set yourself up for success.** Many plants need shelter from wind and animals. Take notice of who might be out to eat your garden before you do, and pinpoint your sunniest locations. Most veggie gardens need full sun (six to eight hours of direct sunlight).

☙ **Get watering right.** Decide how you're going to water your garden before you plant. Drip systems, soaker hoses and nanny pots are generally more effective at watering than we are, and soil-level watering helps prevent disease and conserve water. Once you have a system in place, you'll feel like your garden practically runs itself.

☙ **Copy nature.** In nature, water runs downhill. So, too, should water in your garden. Make sure planters and garden beds have adequate drainage. Tend your soil, adding organic matter to make a healthy home for beneficial soil microbes and decomposers. Plant in polycultures. Diversity will minimize problems with pests and attract pollinators.

☙ **If it ain't broke, don't fix it.** If a plant looks happy, it probably is, and watering or fertilizing it more won't make it happier. In fact, it may do the opposite.

☙ **Keep your garden close.** Place it where you can see it from a window, where you pass by on a daily basis or in a place you like to be. This immediately shifts the garden experience from burden to lifestyle. Time spent tending to it becomes part of everyday living — taking just a few minutes here and there.

☙ **Let go of perfect.** Expect one-hit wonders, consistent winners and losing battles. Don't wait for everything to be just so to start planting — embrace the fact that gardens are the definition of change. Some plants thrive while others die; you and your garden will evolve together.

THE BASIC INGREDIENTS

In a garden, nature is your starting point and with it come many of the ingredients necessary to plant your first seeds and watch them grow. I won't lie and say planting and growing a garden will be effortless, but the rewards make every minute worth it. You may face a myriad of challenges, from weather to seed-eating birds, but these challenges are often incredibly valuable — and have an uncanny way of helping us grow along with our gardens.

Climate

One way to understand plants is to figure out where they're from. As with people, native geography is telling, and with plants, geography tells you their preferred climate.

Climate is place based. Elevation, topography, proximity to water (such as an ocean or lake), wind and latitude all have a hand in affecting climate. Further, rainfall (the amount and timing), humidity, average high and low temperatures and length of the growing season are all products of climate. It's helpful to have a general understanding of these things because they tell you what you can plant and when.

The length of the growing season is the days between the last spring frost and the first fall frost. Knowing when your average annual frost dates land on the calendar helps determine which plant varieties are best to grow, when to plant, whether seeds need to be started indoors and whether you can direct-sow seeds in the garden. For instance, if you're growing tomatoes, which can take 120 days or more to mature from seed to fruit (also known as the days to maturity), and you have a shorter growing season, you'll need to start seeds indoors. Frost dates also help determine when to plant cool-season vegetables, which are often planted weeks before the first fall frost, and in mild climates or climates with cold summer nights, weeks before your last spring frost.

Average annual frost dates vary from year to year but can be used to create a planting schedule. Simply calculate planting times using your last spring frost and first fall frost dates as benchmarks. To get started, determine your hardiness zone using a hardiness zone map, and then consult the following chart. (See hardiness maps, pages 264–265.) Or for more precise dates, use a frost date calculator.

Average Annual Frost Date By Zone

	Average Last Spring Frost	Average First Fall Frost
Zone 1	June 1 - June 30	July 1 - July 31
Zone 2	May 1 - May 31	Aug. 1 - Aug. 31
Zone 3	May 1 - May 31	Sept. 1 - Sept 30
Zone 4	May 1 - May 31	Sept. 1 - Sept 30
Zone 5	March 30 - April 30	Sept. 30 - Oct. 30
Zone 6	March 30 - April 30	Sept. 30 - Oct. 30
Zone 7	March 30 - April 30	Sept. 30 - Oct. 30
Zone 8	Feb. 28 - March 30	Oct. 30 - Nov. 30
Zone 9	Jan. 30 - Feb. 28	Nov. 30 - Dec. 30
Zone 10	Jan 30 - or earlier	Nov. 30 - Dec. 30
Zone 11	Frost free year round	

Hardiness zones are used to compare climate by region and reference the lowest average annual winter temperature for a particular area. They're the basis by which gardeners determine which plants may thrive (or survive) in a particular region. If the region experiences a winter low of -15°F (-26°C) as found in zone 5, plants recommended for that region are generally perennials that can survive these temperatures. The same is true of summer heat — not all plants are adapted to thrive when temperatures rise. A hardiness zone map is an excellent guide when selecting varieties, and you'll often see it referenced on plant tags and seed packets. Use it as a starting point, and remember it's not perfect and there are other factors at play that also affect plant selections, such as soil, drainage, freeze and thaw cycles and rainfall.

A **microclimate** is a climate within a climate. Trees or fences that direct wind, cold sinks that often occur at the base of hillsides, the radiant heat found when

planting near walls, and reflected light can all make a huge difference in how your garden grows. As you plant from one season to the next, move containers around and experiment with different plant varieties — you'll learn the subtleties of your microclimate and be able to use them to your advantage.

Sun

Green things are green thanks to photosynthesis, food-making powered by the sun. The amount of sun needed by individual plants to thrive depends on the type of plant and its unique adaptations. It's critical to understand how much sun you have to work with throughout the day or over a season because it dictates what you can grow. While full sun (six to eight hours of direct sun) is best for most kitchen garden edibles, it's not a requirement. Many rewarding herbs and leafy greens grow in part shade.

Sun vs. Shade

Full sun: Six to eight hours of sun a day. These hours can be continuous or divided.

Part sun and part shade: Three to six hours of sun a day. However, plants labeled part shade grow best with direct morning light and when sheltered from afternoon sun (afternoon sun is generally the most intense).

Shade or full shade: Less than three hours of direct sunlight a day — it's often best if they occur in the morning. Bright but indirect light also falls into this category.

When determining how much sun is available to you, start with aspect. What are the barriers to light? Does your garden sit below a hill, fence, neighboring building or tree line? If there's a barrier to the north, there's a good chance south-facing light is available and full sun along with it, but if it's to the south you're likely working with part-shade or full-shade conditions.

It's also important to remember light intensity changes throughout the day and can often work in your favor. Morning sun (east facing) is the least intense, whereas afternoon sun (west facing) can be harsh and hot. Your garden plot may be on the edge for required full-sun hours, but if it receives the majority of its light in the afternoon, the odds are in your favor for a successful kitchen garden.

Emily's Note

Taking time to cultivate garden soil is the number one thing you can do to grow the most amazing garden possible. What's wonderful is that the steps to cultivating garden soil are fairly simple.

Soil

The healthier your soil the healthier your garden — and the better your fruits and veggies will taste. The exception is perennial herbs and other plants native to the Mediterranean. Mediterranean plants are adapted not only to their particular home climate but also to their home soil, which tends to have a higher ratio of grit to organic matter. In general, it's less nutrient rich and has excellent drainage.

Water

There is rainfall and there is irrigation. (Most regions can't rely solely on rainfall to water their crops.) When considering where you'll plant your garden, consider how it will be watered.

Place your garden or planting containers that require supplemental water as close to a water source as possible. (See page 230, Smart Watering.)

Air

For gardeners, air is usually defined in terms of wind and circulation. It's important for plants to have adequate air circulation for healthy growth, to decrease disease and, for some, to improve pollination success. Understanding wind patterns in your area is key to managing air flow and redirecting heavy winds that can be damaging to plants. Trees, hilling, hedges and fencing can all be used to direct wind and protect crops.

Topography

Wide, open spaces make it simple to plot a garden, manage light and move about to care for your plants. Of course, the ideal garden setting isn't always possible, but hillsides can be tiered, vertical gardens can be constructed, or gardens can meander and change shape with the landscape. In fact, gardens that move and work with the available topography often create an experience that can't be achieved in a neat 8 x 8 square.

The Knoll garden in spring.

Critter Inventory

What animals come to visit your planting area? Do you have trees nearby that double as homes to red-shouldered hawks, owls or chickadees? What do your native pollinators look like? Have you seen cabbage moths flitting by or ladybugs hatching in spring? Assess who lives nearby and may want to eat your prized plants. Do you need to fortify root zones with gopher wire or build barriers to prevent deer from grazing? Curbing the behaviors of some animals, like gophers, is a simple matter of self-preservation. (See page 254 for solutions to unwanted visitors.)

WHERE TO PLANT

The question of where to plant can feel like an ever-moving target, but the best solution is to dig in and see what happens. Keep in mind that plants are forgiving. Expect your garden to change and grow, and your life will be better for it.

Following pages: Raised beds in community garden.

Raised Beds

Raised beds immediately solve a number of problems inherent to gardens. They allow you to focus your attention, defining the space you have to work with; pests can be managed with just a few add-ons, like row cover; and paths are easily defined so there's no need to worry about feet straying into beds and compacting precious soil. Elevating beds also makes them easier to work with, reducing wear and tear on your back and knees.

I find raised beds are most effective when resting directly on the ground, where thermal heat held naturally in soil can be protected and plants can extend roots past the boundary of beds as needed. If there's any question that gophers or voles may come calling, fasten gopher wire or 1/4-inch hardware cloth to the bottom of beds using U nails before filling with soil.

Building a Raised Bed

The size of and materials used to make a raised bed are a product of how you'd like the bed to function and the space you have to dedicate to a garden.

Size

A typical raised bed is often about 4 feet wide and 18 inches tall, with the length determined either by the dimensions of the total garden space or the length of the materials. However, if you're a smaller person or you're designing a garden for children, 4-foot beds may be too wide to reach the center from one side or the other — which is critical. If this is the case, consider beds that are 3 feet or 3 1/2 feet wide.

Longer beds increase your planting area, but they also hold more weight and need to be reinforced. Drive rebar or stakes into soil and fasten them to the interior sides of beds to support them vertically. This reduces the risk of beds bowing or flexing under the pressure and weight of soil as it expands and contracts with the seasons.

Emily's Note

The height of a raised bed is determined by how you plan to use it and what you'd like to grow. If it's lettuces you're after, 12 inches is deep enough. However, if you'd like some flexibility, make it deeper.

Materials

Cinder blocks, stone, galvanized steel and wood are all excellent options and can take on a variety of shapes and sizes. The key is to use materials that are chemical free and don't run the risk of leaching anything harmful into garden soil. I tend to avoid pressure-treated wood or any materials that have held or been treated with chemicals.

Fill beds with the best soil you can find, make or buy. The goal is to have excellent drainage and plenty of organic matter to foster habitat not only for your plants but also for microbes and other tiny animals that constitute a soil life cycle. Begin with an organic mix of compost and topsoil that is as locally sourced as possible. Many landscape supply companies offer a 60:40 or 50:50 mix of compost to topsoil. Start here and add amendments as you grow. (See page 38 for more on soil.)

Container Gardens

It's possible to grow a garden in any number and style of containers. Make planters with wood or by upcycling a tin or wine box. Repurpose a pallet, add drain holes to a trash can or buy planters ready-made at your local nursery. The right-sized container for planting is one you can move around yourself, either by lifting and carrying or by pulling or wheeling.

The trick with container gardening is managing soil, nutrients and moisture. There's a cumulative effect as time passes, plants are watered and amendments are added to containers that causes soil to become denser and less nutrient rich. The

The deck garden.

solution is to start with a light, well-draining potting soil that contains coconut coir for retaining moisture without becoming waterlogged. It's also helpful to repot and change all or a portion of the soil in a container once a year, especially with smaller containers (planters that are 10 gallons in size or less). I like to use compost or manure tea to amend container plantings and occasionally use a granular fertilizer, particularly with citrus, other small fruit trees and blueberries.

Troughs

The next best thing to a raised bed is a galvanized watering trough. They're light and inexpensive, they require little up-front leg work, and they look fabulous. All you need to do is get one home and add drain holes. Cover the bottom with a thin layer of coarse gravel to improve drainage, and then fill it with an organic planting mix. I blend my own soil mix, combining compost and potting soil or a planting mix with coconut coir and rice hulls to ensure I have the lightest, richest soil with excellent structure.

WORKSHOP #1
CONVERT A TROUGH INTO A RAISED BED

First, determine the garden space you have to work with by measuring the outside plot dimensions, then compare this space with standard trough sizes.

Prepare your garden space. Will your trough rest on a bed of gravel or mulch, or a hard surface like a paver patio? If on a patio or deck, it's best to elevate the trough to improve drainage and reduce the wear and tear of your surface. I find wood slats cut to the length of the trough are best. Use at least three for a 2-foot-wide trough so the trough doesn't flex or bow. The slats also make it easy to run irrigation underneath, down the length of the beds, where it's protected and hidden.

Flip your trough over, and use a drill and a 1/4-inch drill bit to add drain holes to the bottom of the trough. Space them about 6 to 8 inches apart.

Fill larger troughs with an inch of drain rock (you'll find it at a landscape supply store), and then add an organic planting mix.

First add drainage

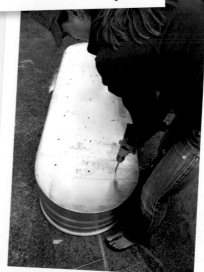
Drill holes

Maybe get a friend to help

Good Old-Fashioned Veggie Plots

To create an in-ground garden, determine where it will go; test your soil for pollution, soil quality and pH (for more on soil testing, see page 42); and then map the outside dimensions of your plot. Now, it's time to dig. I recommend double digging before planting because it will save you a whole lot of headaches later.

Double digging involves a spade, a fork, compost or well-rotted manure, any amendments recommended with soil testing and time. It will ultimately loosen soil, give roots plenty of room and improve drainage and soil quality. Using the spade, first dig a 1- to 2-foot-wide trench the depth of the spade. Move the soil to the end of the plot or off the edge. Fork the soil at the bottom of the trench, add compost and amendments, then work the compost in with the fork. Repeat these steps for the next 1 to 2 feet, and this time top the compost with the topsoil from the previous trench. Continue until you've worked the entire planting area, then use the last pile of soil to fill in the first trench.

SHEET MULCHING

When sheet mulching, you're simply laying a blanket of compostable materials over soil, lawn or particularly precocious weeds. All you need is cardboard and mulch (such as wood chips or bark). Cardboard acts as a biodegradable weed barrier, and mulch repeats this process as well as adding valuable organic matter to soil, making it light and workable.

Roll out a sheet of cardboard or lay flattened cardboard boxes over your garden plot after saturating the soil (or lawn) with water. Make sure the edges of cardboard have plenty of overlap to eliminate gaps. Once the area is covered, spread a 3- to 4-inch layer of mulch over the cardboard and let nature do its work. The length of time it takes to successfully sheet mulch an area depends on your climate and the plants you've just covered. If your lawn was mostly Bermuda grass, it could take a year of sheet mulching (two rounds or more) to remove it. It's possible to sheet mulch any time of year, although I find it's best to begin the process in late summer or fall before winter weather sets in.

GARDENER'S TOOLKIT

It's possible to begin a garden with a container, soil, seeds, a water source and just your hands. However, over the years I've built up a small quiver of tools I reach for frequently and often.

- Like shoes, I wear **gloves** only when I have to. I love to get my hands on things — it's my way of knowing them. A little dirt under my nails reminds me I'm alive.

- When working with tiny things, like seeds and sprouts, I keep a **pencil** or **chopstick** handy. These make the work of transplanting easy.

- I love a good **hand trowel**. I have several and place them strategically, one by the backdoor, another left in a planter and another lumped in with the rest of my tools. It's the same with **clippers**. If I leave them where I can easily find them, I can make quick work of harvesting or emergency pruning. My micro-snips are in with the pencils and the heavy-duty clippers next to the **liquid seaweed** and **twine** — the other two things I reach for on a regular basis.

🪶 I find a good **mattock** incredibly helpful when doing the work of weeding and tending to soil. Next is a good old-fashioned **spade** and a **garden fork** for the heavier work of moving soil and turning compost.

🪶 **Buckets**, **bamboo stakes**, **watering cans** of different sizes and flows, and a **wheelbarrow** all come in handy.

🪶 Having a **hose** and knowing where your **hose bib** or water main is are essential.

KNOW THE RULES SO YOU CAN BREAK THEM

Don't listen to anyone who says your garden needs to look like this or that, not even me. Think of garden-making as an opportunity to tell your story. Plants, dirt and the food you grow and cook are your pen and paper — and you're the author. As with anything creative, the best art comes from reaching past what you thought possible.

In the garden, some rules are critical. They keep your plants alive and your garden in tip-top shape, which means more of everything for you — more food, more flowers, more fun. But when you're planning your garden and figuring out how to optimize space or where to grow your plants, the rules are a starting point, so bend them as you see fit.

LAYING THE GROUNDWORK: CULTIVATING SOIL & COMPOSTING

For many of us, soil is mysterious. We're still learning about the complex relationships found underground, from the soil food web to the countless symbiotic interactions between plants, animals, fungi and bacteria. Yet although the world of soil may seem like uncharted territory, there are just a handful of principles to keep in mind when cultivating it to support healthy, thriving plants.

What You Should Know Before Cultivating

- Organic is best. Steer clear of pesticides, herbicides and chemical fertilizers, which interrupt natural life cycles above and below ground.

- Soil is alive. It's the heart of the garden and requires care and attention. The better your soil, the better the food you grow will taste.

- When making compost and amending your garden, use local materials: scraps from your kitchen, leaves from your trees, droppings from the neighbors' chickens.

- Compost liberally — top-dressing with compost, leaves and organic-rich ingredients is the best method for mimicking nature.

KNOW YOUR SOIL

Soil health, structure, type and pH are all key when it comes to preparing the ground for your garden. First, figure out what you're working with and then look for ways to feed the soil. Alter pH as needed, and choose a composting system that's best for you.

Healthy Soil

You know soil is healthy if it supports life. In between the soil particles, which are really just varying amounts of grit, rock dust, minerals and broken-down organic matter like leaves, twigs and poop, is life — soil should be teeming with microbes, fungi, worms and critters of all kinds.

When the plant directory calls for rich, well-draining soil, I'm referring to soil that is balanced and nutrient rich because of a high ratio of organic matter (like manure, leaves and other compost components), and also to soil that holds a range of the nutrients plants need to thrive.

Plants, like people, require an assortment of macro- and micronutrients to successfully carry out the work of growing from seed to fruit. Nitrogen (N), phosphorus (P) and potassium (K) are the heavy hitters. When you see *NPK* on a bag of soil or a box of fertilizer, these are the key elements, although equally important are calcium, magnesium, sulfur, oxygen and carbon.

Good soil is full of life.

To understand what you're working with, dig in and have a look. What happens when you squeeze a handful of soil and then let it go? If it's in good shape, it will hold together for a moment and then gently come apart and look light and fluffy in the palm of your hand.

Soil Structure and Tilth

Think of soil as being made up of four basic building blocks: sand, silt, clay and humus (organic matter). Sand, silt and clay are all varying sizes of sediment. Clay soil particles are the smallest and the most dustlike, adhering tightly to one another. Sand is more granular. It's easy to feel sand when you mix water with a pinch of soil and stir it around in your hand with a finger. Silt is in between; its particles are larger than those of clay and smaller than sand. Combine an equal mix of these ingredients with organic matter (the food and product of living things), and you have the makings for a healthy soil, called loam.

It's not common for a soil to be a perfect mix, which is why it's often described as being heavy clay, sandy or some version of the three. Clay is good at holding nutrients, but it can be dense and difficult to work and is often wet or waterlogged. A sandy soil is ideal for many drought-tolerant plants and is free-draining, but generally not nutrient rich.

Most edibles prefer rich, loamy soils with excellent tilth. They're light, airy and easy to work. Making and adding compost to soil is the best and easiest way to maintain soil tilth. Compacting soil by walking on it; not mulching or protecting soil, especially during rainy seasons; and working soil when it's overly wet are some of the fastest ways to have an impact on soil tilth.

Organic Matter

One of the most important benefits of amending your garden with compost is that it adds organic matter, which breaks down into small particles called humus. In sandy soil, these particles get between the sand particles and act like sponges, holding both nutrients and water in the soil. In clay soils organic matter helps break apart the lumps of clay, making them more permeable to both water and the tiny feeder roots of the plants. Humus also protects soil from drastic shifts in pH.

Emily's Note

To test soil structure, wet a small handful and try to create a thin ribbon. Shape the soil by forming it between your thumb and forefinger or by rolling it between the palms of your hands. If it makes a ribbon that doesn't fall apart, you're working with clay soil. If it forms a ribbon but then falls apart when you touch or bend it, you're working with loam. If it doesn't form a ribbon at all, your soil is sandy.

Soil pH

The acidity or alkalinity of soil is measured as pH. On the pH scale, a reading of 7 is neutral, while readings below 7 are acidic and readings above are alkaline. Determining soil pH is critical because plants have optimal pH ranges within which they can successfully take up and assimilate nutrients through their roots.

Most plants prefer fairly neutral soils ranging from 6 to 7. However, there are some, like blueberries and their cousins, that prefer acidic soils ranging between 4 and 5. You can tell if your soil leans toward acidic or alkaline by the plants that are already growing in your neighborhood. If you see azaleas or rhododendrons, the parent soil is most likely acidic or slightly acidic. Plants such as lilac, hydrangea and honeysuckle prefer alkaline soils.

There are kits designed for home use or labs that will do the job of analyzing soil for you. When sending a sample out for testing, request a reading on soil pH, contaminants and nutrient value, and also ask for organic soil amendment recommendations. (If you don't specify organic amendment recommendations, most labs will send chemical fertilizer recommendations.)

Amending Soil pH

It's nearly impossible to alter the soil pH of an entire garden, but targeting specific areas based on what you're growing can be highly effective. If you'd like to make an acid soil more alkaline, add lime. Bringing an acid soil closer to neutral or alkaline will also increase the activity of worms and beneficial bacteria. Because lime doesn't last long in soil, you may need to apply it regularly. The easiest way to make soil more acidic is by using peat moss, but peat isn't sustainable, so I recommend using sulfur products instead.

Manure tea time

NPK Basics

Nitrogen (N), phosphorus (P) and potassium (K) are the three core elements required by plants to live and grow.

Nitrogen is part of chlorophyll and a key player in the photosynthetic process. You can tell that plants need nitrogen when their leaves yellow and growth is slow. Organic sources of nitrogen include composted manure, manure tea, fish emulsion, amendments made from soy and alfalfa, and a crop rotation of legumes.

Phosphorus also has a role in photosynthesis and is vital for abundant flower and fruit development. When leaves look bluish, plants have fewer blooms and fruits are not well developed or taste acidic, it's time to give them a boost of phosphorus. A top dressing of compost, compost tea, worm castings and bone meal are all good phosphorus amendments.

Potassium is vital to the overall strength and health of plants, helping them boost resistance to pests and disease. You know your plants need potassium when leaf tips curl, leaf veins yellow and leaves develop purple or brown spots. Start with compost and worm castings to fix the problem, although ash, kelp, seaweed meal and greensand are other potassium amendments that will help.

SOIL BUILDING AND COMPOSTING

You know that wonderfully rich, earthy smell of great soil? It's actually not the soil you're smelling, but the bacteria living in the soil. Bacteria do the work of decomposing most everything we throw at them: grass clippings, leaves, green waste and food scraps. They eat and poop and, in the process, make the finest compost we can give our gardens. Feed your garden for free by making something wonderful with things you might otherwise throw away.

The added beauty of compost is that it's a delivery system of nutrients and organic matter plants recognize and can easily assimilate. While most composts don't rank high in NPK, it's not the concentration or quantity of these nutrients that matter, but the quality. Compost is our best method of mimicking nature.

Make Your Own Compost

There's more than one method for making compost, but no matter the process the goal is the same: to create habitat for decomposers. Give them food, water, air and shelter and they'll flourish.

Cold Compost

Cold composting is the simplest method and ideal for fall composting, when cold winter temperatures naturally slow the decomposition process. It's a fix-it-and-forget-it pile. Stack together carbon- and nitrogen rich-ingredients such as green waste from your yard, kitchen scraps and leaves to make a pile that is ideally 3 x 3 x 3 feet in size. (The smaller the pile the longer it will take, and the larger the pile the harder it is to work with it.) Give it a helping of water so it's moist, but not soggy, and walk away. You can speed up the process by tossing a handful of garden soil into the mix (healthy garden soil contains decomposers) and by turning the pile occasionally, but it's not necessary. In general, cold-composted materials take about nine months to a year to form soil.

HOT COMPOST

With a little more care, you can create a compost pile that gets nice and hot, killing weed seeds and making soil in just one to three months.

What You Need

Browns. Twigs, sticks, straw, dried grass or leaves, shredded newspaper, cardboard, sawdust, wood ash.

Greens. Kitchen scraps, yard waste, garden trimmings, grass clippings, manure.

Soil. Soil from garden beds or finished compost.

Water. Moisten your compost pile so it's damp but not saturated. A compost pile that is overly wet will become home to anaerobic bacteria and begin to smell.

Air. Turn your pile periodically to add air to the mix.

Avoid adding meats, oily foods, dairy, weeds, diseased plant material, products containing chemicals or pesticides, and cat or dog poop to your compost pile.

What You Do

- The fastest way to make compost is to chop or shred brown and green materials. The smaller the pieces, the faster they'll decompose. Run a lawn mower over leaves and small twigs to break them down.
- Wait until you have enough materials to make an initial pile that's at least 3 square feet in size. Once you have your materials gathered, it's time to cook.
- Layer materials by first adding 6 to 7 inches of browns. I put the coarsest materials, such as twigs and small branches, on the bottom to ensure there's plenty of air flow moving from the bottom to top of the pile.

- Next, top the browns with a 3- to 4-inch layer of greens. Sprinkle a thin layer of soil or finished compost over these two layers, and then repeat again with browns, then greens, then soil, and so on, showering each layer with water as you go. You're essentially adding browns and greens in a 2:1 ratio, which is something to keep in mind when you continue adding to it over time.

- If you're composting outside a bin or container, do your best to maintain a rectangular pile, which keeps it upright and even along the edges.

- Mix the layers together by stirring your compost pile with a garden fork. To get your pile cooking and hot, stir it once a week. You can continue adding kitchen scraps to the early stages of your pile once it's made. Just tuck them in under a layer of browns, or add browns over the top of the greens and sprinkle with water.

- When your pile feels warm in the center or it reads 150°F (66°C) on a compost thermometer, you know it's time to turn it. Turning it when it's warm helps speed the decomposition process.

- Your compost is ready to go out to the garden when it no longer gives off heat and it's dry, fluffy and looks like garden soil.

Opposite: If it's plant-based with no added chemicals, it's compostable. Below: Avocado thriving in the compost pile.

Troubleshooting

- The heat generated by a compost pile is a sign of bacteria and other decomposers at work. If your pile isn't gaining in temperature, it needs more green materials and oxygen. Add food scraps and other greens, and turn it more frequently.

- If your pile is smelly and slimy, it's too wet. Mix in brown materials and aerate it well. If your pile is dry, add moisture and mix it well.

- Starting your pile in late spring allows you to take advantage of summer heat. External heat naturally speeds the process of decay, and you can have finished compost in just a few short months.

- If rodents are a problem, consider wrapping wood bins with 1/4-inch hardware cloth and adding a lid, or use enclosed bins. It's also possible to deter rodents and other animals from your pile by stirring it often and not adding breads, cooked food and rich-smelling food scraps like banana peels.

WORM COMPOSTING

If you have room under your kitchen sink or in your garage, mudroom or garden for a small box or tub, you have room to compost with worms. They're incredibly easy to care for given the right environment, and you get worm poop (vermicompost, aka black gold) in exchange for food scraps, leaves and water.

Set up a worm bin in a wood box or plastic container. Make your own worm home, or purchase one already made. Wood is heavy and less easy to shift or move as needed, but it's breathable and renewable. I find wood bins are best if you can dedicate a space in your yard that's shaded throughout the year. Plastic containers hold moisture well, making it easy to capture precious worm "tea," and are light and mobile. They're a good choice for both indoor and outdoor use.

*It's difficult to think anything but pleasant thoughts
while eating a homegrown tomato.*
— LEWIS GIZZARD

the PLANT
DIRECTORY

TENDER HERBS

BASIL, PARSLEY, DILL, CILANTRO, CHERVIL

You've probably heard this before: "If you're going to grow anything, grow herbs." And it's true. Herbs offer the biggest bounty from the smallest of gardens. You can harvest what you need when you need it (no more forgotten bundles of parsley liquefying at the bottom of your crisper), and the potential to elevate the flavor of everyday meals is immediate. Plus, there are flowers — I sometimes think they're the best part. When you buy herbs at the market, their flowers usually haven't yet formed, or they've been discarded. Although they may not have the same nutritional value as leaves, the flavor of herbal flowers is often just as vibrant.

Annual herbs give you flexibility with how and where you grow them. Because they live their lives within a single season, their root systems require less room than their perennial counterparts. They can also thrive in small spaces and containers that could fit perfectly on a stair landing or window ledge.

Basil or Sweet Basil

Ocimum basilicum

One of the most versatile herbs of the mint family with countless varieties, sweet basil has incredible influence on flavor. Growing your own gives you room to experiment and discover a whole new set of possibilities — beyond pesto.

Give basil plenty of sunlight, rich soil and water, and you'll have a happy plant that, when well pruned, keeps on giving. I generally pair it in the garden with heat lovers like tomatoes and plants with similar water and light requirements, like zucchini and cucumbers. You can also grow it solo in its own container so it's easy to bring in and out of the house.

Plant

SUN, REGULAR WATERING

Annual. Plant from seed or starts. Start seeds indoors about four to six weeks before day- and nighttime temperatures are at or above 50°F (10°C). Sow seeds approximately 1/4 inch deep. (See page 218 for seed-sowing tips.) Plant out when day and night temperatures are at or above 50°F. Plant 8 inches apart, and plant dwarf varieties 4 inches apart when starts are approximately 6 inches tall. Grows about 1 to 1 1/2 feet tall.

Grow basil from seed if you want hard-to-find varieties, you have visions of pesto, or you'd like to grow it year-round indoors and out. However, it can be helpful and cost effective to purchase starts at your local nursery, especially if you plan to grow only one or two plants. Just test the fragrance of the plant first by rubbing the leaves between your fingers — you'll immediately get a sense of how flavorful it will be.

Basil prefers rich, fertile soil and grows best when soil temperatures hover around 70°F (21°C). Give plants plenty of sun and heat. There's no need to overfeed or fertilize as this can affect the final flavor. For occasional use, grow one or two plants. To have enough for pesto, grow six or more.

Emily's Note

The variety of basil and the size of its leaves affect flavor, pungency and aromatic qualities. Experiment with different varieties, or nibble the leaves of nursery starts before buying to be sure it's the flavor for you.

Pick

Get more from your basil through harvesting — the more you pick, the more it grows.

Begin by pinching off the tips of terminal stems that have three or four sets of true leaves. This will help your plant grow fuller, promoting continued growth. Harvest this way throughout the growing season.

For pesto, pinch tips to promote branching and prevent flower formation. Once your plants are about 12 to 18 inches tall, harvest up to two-thirds of the plant, leaving three or four sets of leaves. Prune just above the leafing points to encourage plants to continue growing.

Harvest the entire plant before the first frost or when you see leaves beginning to drop. (Leaf drop is a sign that temperatures are dipping below optimal range.) Try bringing your plants indoors to extend the growing season.

Fix

Basil pairs well with summer vegetables, such as tomatoes, zucchini, new potatoes, greens of any kind and eggplant. Plop a sprig into your summer cocktail; add it to salad dressings, soups and fruit jams; or use as a garnish on fish or roasted vegetables. Try pairing it with thyme, rosemary and mint (I especially love basil with mint in summer rolls made straight from the garden). It's also lovely with cheese and anything that involves tomatoes. Add basil to recipes at the last minute because cooking affects flavor.

Varieties to Try

African Blue. One of my favorite companion plants (see page 245), this frost-sensitive perennial hybrid smells like mint and camphor. It's not commonly used in cooking, but you can experiment with it in small amounts or as a dried herb.

'Cinnamon.' This variety has a warm cinnamon flavor and fragrance, with hints of cloves and anise.

'Genovese.' This sweet basil is a quintessential pesto ingredient.

'Holy basil,' or **'Tulsi.'** Revered in India and considered sacred, it's often used in Asian food and teas for its restorative properties.

'Mrs. Burns.' This basil tastes and smells of lemon. Use it when you want to enhance rich, citrus flavors.

'Purple Dark Opal' and **'Purple Petra.'** Their purple leaves are sweetly pungent, with hints of clove and ginger.

'Queenette.' A true Thai basil, it's anise-scented and slightly spicy. Try it in cocktails, canning and sauces.

'Windowbox Mini.' This sweet basil fits perfectly in a small container or window box, where it's easy to harvest leaves.

Parsley

Petroselinum hortense

Of all the herbs, it's parsley I use most. It's an everyday staple, and while you can buy it at the market, there's a certain joy in knowing it's growing close by. Like an old friend whose qualities I've come to trust, I know parsley will give the simplest dishes a depth of flavor that would otherwise be missed. I generally grow flat-leaf over curly as its leaves are easy to work with and I find its flavor more robust.

Plant

SUN OR PART SHADE. MODERATE TO REGULAR WATER.

Biennial. Plant from seed or starts. Slow to germinate but not tricky to grow from seed. Quicken germination by presoaking seeds for 12 to 24 hours before planting. Sow seeds approximately 1/4 inch deep when weather is cool. If you're planting outdoors, sow four to six weeks before last average frost; for indoors, sow six to eight weeks before last average frost. Maintain moist soil during germination process. Grow year-round in mild climates, and space about 8 inches apart when planting out. Grows 12 to 18 inches tall.

While parsley grows easily from seed, you may want to begin with a seedling. Seeds can take up to a month to emerge from the soil, and it can seem like an eternity. Like basil, you may need only one or two plants to get started. If you *do* grow parsley from seed, consider sharing any surplus with a friend or neighbor as it's often difficult to use the entire packet before the expiration date.

Tuck parsley in between other plants to protect it from the summer sun, or plant in part shade if growing in a hot climate. It likes moist soil, and you'll find it grows best if the soil doesn't dry out. Use a rich, well-draining soil for best results.

Pick

Harvest parsley when it's grown about 10 to 12 leaves. Unlike basil, count the leaves by counting the stems growing up from the ground at the base of the plant. When harvesting, cut the stem at soil level to encourage new growth. Harvest what you need when you need it, and continue harvesting until your plant goes to seed or loses its flavor and becomes tough.

Fix

Eat leaves and stems, or just the leaves and save the stems for soup stocks. I keep a container in my freezer where I collect unused bits of vegetables for making soup stock. Once the container is full, cook it down by covering the end pieces with water. Bring it to a boil, reduce heat and simmer for about 90 minutes and then strain. Or, depending on what you've saved and the flavor you're after, sauté the veggie bits with onion before simmering in a pot of water. This way nothing goes to waste and your soups will taste amazing.

Parsley's savory nature complements nearly every dish. It's a perfect counterpart to sweet vegetables and adds depth to soups, sauces, dressings and grain-based salads.

> ### Emily's Note
>
> Swallowtail butterflies lay their eggs on plants like parsley, dill and fennel. Look for their yellow and black larvae or caterpillars in spring — maybe your garden will become a butterfly habitat!

Dill

When I was 9, I spent many summer days working with my fifth grade teacher on her tiny homestead. We trellised cane berries and planted row after row of cucumbers and dill. When they came in, we canned jar after jar of pickles. This is when I got to know dill up close and personal, although it was only later that I fell in love with it tossed in fresh salads or sprinkled over potatoes.

One of the more popular varieties is 'Bouquet,' which boasts good leaf production and gorgeous flowers. It's perfect for pickling and everyday cooking. A dwarf variety like 'Fernleaf' grows well in containers, has high leaf yields and is slow to bolt.

Plant

SUN. REGULAR WATER.

Annual. Plant from seed. Direct-sow whenever possible as soon as soil can be worked. Requires light to germinate. When sowing seeds, simply press into soil surface. Thin to 6-inch spacing for best results. Likes rich, well-draining soil. Mature height varies depending on variety and climate.

If you're planning a pickling garden, try sowing seeds in late April or early May for your best chance of timing it with other fruits or veggies. Or, for general use, plant successionally starting as early as March in warmer climates, and sow every three weeks through August for a continuous supply of greens. Dill grows best if protected from wind and can handle light frost.

Pick

Dill leaves are packed with flavor and can be harvested at any time; however, plants will have the most leaves before it sets flower. Pinch off individual leaves as you need them, or remove entire stems. Dry surplus leaves to make dill weed by spreading them out in a cool, shady location with good circulation. To harvest and save

seeds for later use, let the flowers mature, and harvest seed heads right when the flowers fall away. Place in a paper bag, let dry, then shake the seeds loose inside the bag. When pickling, harvest the entire plant when the flowers are in bloom or when seeds are half ripe (a little green, before they turn brown).

Fix

The eating possibilities are endless: Try pairing dill with tomatoes, green beans, squash, cucumbers, potatoes, carrots, beets, corn and eggs. It's lovely mixed with soft cheese and, of course, pickles. Add it to savory homemade breads and scones, and sprinkle into soups. Eat it fresh in salads, use it as a garnish, or, one of my favorites, whip up some Mexican potato salad.

Cilantro

Coriandrum sativum

I'm a cilantro lover, although I know there are generally two camps of people: those who love it and those who don't. It has real wow factor and can take over the taste of other foods, depending on its use. I often grow it with leaf lettuces and other cut-and-come-again greens for easy harvesting, or I tuck it in between green beans or behind tomatoes to protect it from midsummer heat.

Cilantro is quick to bolt, but the flowers are edible and pollinators love them.

Plant

SUN. REGULAR WATER.

Annual. Direct-sow seeds between two weeks before last average frost and three weeks before first fall frost. Seed-planting depth is 1/4 to 1/2 inch. Thin to 6 inches between seedlings using scissors. Prefers moderately rich, well-draining soil and regular moisture. Grows in cooler temperatures. Grows 12 to 18 inches tall.

Cilantro germinates easily when directly sown and soils aren't left to dry out during the germination process. It generally doesn't transplant well, but that's okay because there are more varieties to choose from when growing from seed. Look for slow-bolting varieties such as 'Long Standing' as they tend to have the longest lifespans.

Market-bought cilantro tends to bruise easily, and growing it yourself gives you flexibility, ease of use and fabulous flavor. Plan to sow seeds successively every three weeks for a full season of greens, or let it reseed itself when it goes to flower.

Pick

Harvesting begins with your thinnings. Think of them as microgreens. What is clipped out with scissors to make room for larger plants to grow can be used on a sandwich or eaten on the spot. Clip individual leaves or sprigs of leaves to use as needed. Harvesting will help ward off bolting, although this can't be avoided with cilantro. (It will eventually bolt, especially when temperatures rise.) Add the flowers to vases, let them go to seed to begin another crop, or collect them and save the seeds for cooking.

Fix

There's something wonderful about eating cilantro on the spot or dashing to the garden and harvesting a few leaves to toss into a salad right before serving. Try it with roasted veggies like carrots if you don't have chervil or parsley, and use it to season sauces. You can also pair it with citrus, or add it to salsa or anything spicy or in need of zest.

Chervil

Anthriscus cerefolium

Delicate, pretty and another cousin of parsley, chervil is one of the four *fines herbes* of France (a group of herbs — parsley, chives, tarragon and chervil — considered essential for cooking). While revered in Europe, it's less known in North America and can be hard to find at the market. Chervil makes other flavors in a dish come to life. Use it where you're looking for hints of tarragon, anise and parsley, although it doesn't replace parsley.

Plant

SUN OR PART SHADE. MODERATE TO REGULAR WATER.

Annual. Grow from seed as it doesn't transplant well. Direct-sow seeds 1/4 inch deep, and thin seedlings to 4 to 6 inches apart. Plant in early spring or late summer. Grow in rich, moist soil. Grows best when temperatures are cool; bolts in hot weather. Takes light frost.

Tuck chervil in between other plants to protect it from direct sun, or grow where it will naturally have protection while still receiving light. It prefers evenly moist soil and some fertilizing with an organic, nitrogen-rich amendment. Sow every few weeks for a continual harvest, or treat it as a seasonal food (spring and early summer).

Pick

Encourage leaf production with pruning. When plants are about 4 inches tall, cut them back to near the ground, leaving just enough leaves to continue growing. Harvest older leaves as they grow, and if it looks as though it's going to bolt, take the entire plant from the ground up.

Fix

Use chervil while it's fresh, adding it to dishes at the last minute. It can take some heat — in fact, this can bring out its flavor — but there's a fine line between just enough and too much, so be careful. It will quickly lose its flavor if overheated.

Chervil works well in savory dishes and salads and with eggs and fish. Try adding it to sauces, juices and soups, or other dishes with sorrel or spinach. Freeze any surplus for later use as it doesn't hold its flavor when dried.

Mix & Match Pesto

Years ago when studying herbal medicine, I discovered you could throw nearly any edible green into a blender with nuts, olive oil, garlic, Parmesan cheese and salt and pepper and it would taste amazing — that is, as long as the greens were flavorful from the beginning. Once when I was out foraging for herbs for teas, I found a fabulous patch of sheep sorrel (a weed to most but a lucky find for me). I gathered what I could and made the most wonderful pesto.

Sheep sorrel is loaded with oxalic acid much like French sorrel, which gives both their vibrant, tangy flavor, and it pairs well with parsley, which grounds brighter flavors. This recipe is an experiment in the making and one that can really never go wrong. I suggest taking notes in the sidebar of this book or adding a card to your recipe box with the combinations you try as you make them. These notes will help guide your what-to-plant list and come in handy on the days when you don't know what to fix for dinner but you're craving something magical.

What You Need
5 cups leaves such as basil, cilantro, parsley, arugula, mint, perpetual spinach or other greens
1/4 cup nuts such as walnuts, almonds or hazelnuts
1/4 cup pine nuts
3 to 5 garlic cloves (I go light on garlic to make it family friendly, but if you're a garlic fanatic, add more)
1 tsp. each freshly ground salt and pepper
1 1/2 cups extra-virgin olive oil (the best you can find or afford)
1 cup grated Parmesan cheese

What You Do
1. Wash and soak greens in a bowl of cold water for 5 minutes or more. Remove tough stems and spin dry.
2. Combine nuts and garlic in a blender or food processor. Chop for about 30 seconds. Once combined, add leaves and salt and pepper.
3. Slowly pour in a portion of the oil and puree. Continue this process until all the olive oil is mixed in with the leaves and other ingredients and your pesto is fairly smooth in consistency. Add the Parmesan, and blend until evenly mixed.
4. Use right away. Add it to salad dressings, or pair it with polenta, pasta, pizza and homemade scones or bread. Refrigerate or freeze extra pesto in an airtight container.

Makes about 5 cups.

PERENNIAL HERBS

MINT, OREGANO AND MARJORAM,
ROSEMARY, SAGE, THYME

Every so often, a story breaks that changes the way you see the world. For me, it was a story about Acciaroli, a village in Italy where one in 10 residents lives to be 100. People there live healthy, relatively illness-free lives. Many walk where they need to go and grow their own food when they can. They also eat rosemary every day. I wondered, could it be as simple as that? Maybe.

Rosemary is a powerful antioxidant and anti-inflammatory. While it's popular in Acciaroli, it's not the only potentially life-changing herb out there. Oregano is the latest cure-all, and thyme and sage share many of the same properties as rosemary.

These herbs are a quiet celebration of all that's good in a garden. They do what they do whether you notice them or not: growing in the toughest places, requiring little attention and thriving all the same. If you're looking for simple ways to make everyday meals a little more extraordinary and add happiness and health to your life, it could be as simple as growing a sprig of rosemary.

Mint

Mentha spp.

This energetic herb practically grows itself and is a must for your "what-to-plant" list. It offers a myriad of flavor combinations and is a pollinator favorite.

Plant

PART SUN TO SUN. MODERATE TO REGULAR WATER.

Perennial. Grow from starts or from stem or root cuttings. Prefers light, free-draining soil. It tolerates cold, growing in USDA hardiness zones 3 to 11. Plant as soon as soil can be worked, and space plants about 12 inches apart, depending on variety and spreading habits. Grows 1 to 2 feet tall with white to purple flowers.

Emily's Note

When left to flower, perennial herbs are overachievers in the companion plant category, and bees, butterflies and hummingbirds relish their blooms.

As wonderful as mint is, it can also be downright intolerable when left to run wild. Grow chocolate mint, spearmint, peppermint and lavender mint to your heart's content, but whatever you do, grow it in containers and don't throw it in your compost. Composting mint risks spreading it throughout your garden as you mulch, and if you add it to your raised beds or veggie plot, it will take over and you'll be weeding it out forever.

Pick

Harvest mint by removing a few leaves or sprigs at a time. Pinch leaves near the base of the leaf, where the leaf stem or petiole attach, or gather sprigs by taking cuttings just above the next branching or leaf point to guarantee a continual harvest throughout the growing season.

Mint can be sheared back at either the end or beginning of your growing season in spring or fall to keep it tidy and encourage growth. Clean up any dead wood, out-of-control branches and old growth to keep it fresh and productive.

Fix

Add mint to pesto, sautéed summer veggies, sun tea, desserts, popsicles and salad dressings. It's just as fabulous with fresh fruit as it is with seasonal greens, fava beans or mojitos. Pair it with lemon or basil, sprinkle it over grilled vegetables, fold it into a frittata or use it to make a simple syrup for your favorite summer cocktail.

Oregano and Marjoram
Origanum spp.

It's no wonder *Origanum* translates as "bright mountain" or that it's long been an essential culinary staple. Intriguing and complex in flavor, oregano has a way of making food come alive. It's easy to love, both for flavor and visual appeal, especially when it's flowering and the bees and butterflies come to visit. The big question with oregano is which variety should you grow?

Plant

SUN. MODERATE TO OCCASIONAL WATER.

Perennial. Grow from cuttings or nursery starts for more immediate use. Requires free-draining soil. Cold hardy, growing in USDA hardiness zones 4 to 10, depending on species. Spacing also depends on the variety. Grows 6 inches to 2 feet. Some nursery plants are grown as ornamentals rather than as culinary herbs.

The flowers of oregano are edible and are just as lovely as the leaves.

Oregano, like thyme, can be grown from seed, but you may want to plant nursery starts or take cuttings from the plants of friends to ensure you're growing the flavors you love most (see how to propagate on page 226). This way you can test the fragrance, and thus the flavor, before investing valuable garden space.

Pick

It doesn't take much to flavor summer dishes, so harvest what you need when you need it. Cut entire stems before they bloom, and hang them to dry in a spot with good air circulation that's out of direct sunlight. It's possible to harvest as much as half the plant at a time — you'll get more from your plants in the long run when they're pruned with some care.

Fix

Use fresh or dried leaves in cooking. Marjoram's sweeter floral flavors pair well with summer dishes. Season zucchini, eggplant, tomatoes, green beans and corn the way you would with basil. Greek oregano is stronger, pungent and slightly bitter and brings foods to life with a bit of force, but it is welcoming all the same. It's the flavor of Italian and Greek cooking, pizzas and lasagna. It pairs well with nearly every vegetable. Beans, meats, salads, sauces and dressings all benefit from a little oregano.

Varieties to Try

Greek oregano. Complex and robust, this variety is prized for its spicy, pungent, yet slightly sweet flavor. White flowers. Grows 12 to 18 inches tall and wide.

Sicilian oregano. This pleasant mix of Greek oregano and marjoram flavors is mildly pungent and sweet. White flowers. Grows 12 to 18 inches tall and wide.

Marjoram. Delicate, sweet and somewhat floral in flavor. Flowers are white to purple or pink. Grows 12 to 18 inches tall and wide. Frost sensitive. Hardy in USDA zones 9 and 10.

Mexican oregano. Not a true oregano, this member of the verbena family is stronger and more bitter in flavor than Greek oregano and is typically used in Mexican cuisine. White flowers. Can grow up to 4 feet tall. Perennial in USDA zones 10 and 11.

Wild marjoram. Not often used as a culinary herb but is highly regarded for its medicinal value. Pink to purple flowers. Grows 12 to 30 inches tall and wide.

Rosemary
Rosmarinus officinalis

My mother always had rosemary growing somewhere in her garden. My grandparents did too. So, of course, all my gardens have included rosemary. Bees come from far and wide, lured in by its lavender blue flowers. Butterflies and hummingbirds love them too. When the plants are in bloom, you can hear the bees before you can see them, flitting from one flower to the next. I once came across a hedge of rosemary that was alive with the sound of contented buzzing.

Plant

SUN. OCCASIONAL WATER.

Perennial. Grow from cuttings or nursery starts for more immediate use. (Consider mixing an organic cactus mix with potting soil.) Thrives in warmer climates, hardiness zones 8 to 11. Overwinter indoors in colder climates. Space plants 1 to 2 feet apart. Grows 2 to 4 feet tall and often wider if left to itself.

As long as rosemary has plenty of sun and the right soil, you can ignore it and it will continue to thrive. One rosemary plant is generally enough for a family, but it also makes a lovely landscaping plant. There are upright and decumbent varieties, so you can use it as a hedge plant in warmer climates or grow it to cascade over stones in a rock garden.

Pick

Gather branches, the ends of stems and flowers as you need them, and try to be strategic with your harvesting, giving your plant shape as you make your cuts (rosemary can quickly outgrow its space and become ungainly if not pruned regularly).

Fix

Use the leaves, stems and flowers when cooking, tossing in entire sprigs or just the leaves themselves. Grind leaves into a paste with other perennial herbs to make a fresh rub for roast turkey or other meats. The branches make perfect aromatic skewers for grilling. Pairs well with roast veggies, potatoes and squash. Try adding it to breads, fruits and desserts for fun — just be careful to use only a little to enhance flavor or it may take over.

Sage
Salvia officinalis

I often think I could grow a garden entirely of sage. It could be an area all its own dedicated to the multiple varieties, hues and scents and would include common garden sage as well as pineapple sage, both of which are beautiful in the garden and indispensable in the kitchen.

Plant

SUN. MODERATE TO OCCASIONAL WATER.

Perennial. Slow to develop from seed; grow from cuttings by layering, or use nursery starts. Requires free-draining soil. Cold hardy, growing in USDA hardiness zones 5 to 10 depending on variety, though doesn't like the humidity of warmer climates. Space plants about 12 inches or more apart. Grows 1 to 3 feet tall and wide.

Adaptable yet doesn't tolerate constantly wet soil. Pair common garden sage with other Mediterranean plants, or place at the edge of beds, away from direct watering by irrigation. It's best to water deeply and occasionally and let soil dry in between waterings.

Pick

Gather leaves to use right away, or dry them to prevent them from turning black. Give plants a healthy pruning in spring to enliven new growth and give plants shape. Fill vases with the flowers — or just eat them!

Fix

This plant changes with the seasons: light and minty in spring, hearty and savory in the fall — just in time for cozy winter dishes. Pair with seasonal fruits and vegetables accordingly. Mince leaves (dried sage is more pungent than fresh) and cook them with olive oil and garlic, adding the combination to almost anything: eggs, cheeses, breads and pasta. Or fry whole leaves in a bit of olive oil until they change color and become crispy. Crumble over pastas, soups, meats and beans. Savor as a restorative tea. Use as a garnish, and experiment with its unique flavor where you might otherwise use mint or lemon.

Thyme

Thymus vulgaris

If you've added freshly chopped thyme to pasta or roasted vegetables, you know that even a small handful adds a wealth of flavor. Common thyme, also known as English thyme, is a good place to start. Lemon thyme performs just as well in the kitchen as it does in the garden. The more water you give thyme, the less flavor it tends to have, so be sure to pair it with other drought-tolerant plants.

Plant

SUN. MODERATE TO OCCASIONAL WATER.

Perennial. Grow from cuttings or nursery starts for more immediate use. Requires free-draining soil. Cold hardy, growing in USDA hardiness zones 5 to 10. Spacing depends on the variety. Grows 6 to 15 inches tall.

Thyme is incredibly reliable and grows well in perennial borders or containers. It can survive some of the harshest of winters under a blanket of snow but thrives just as easily in warmer climates. I've grown it as much for landscaping as I have for cooking. One plant can be enough for a single family, although I find I'm always making room for more.

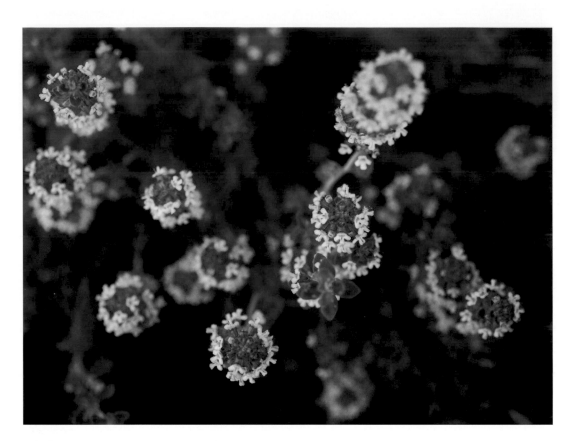

Pick

Harvest entire stems as needed, cutting them away from the plant near the base or just above a branching point (see Pruning, page 235.) Both stem and leaves are packed with flavor, but if you're using only the leaves and they're fairly dry, simply run your fingers down the spine of the stem to release them. Harvest more vigorously if you're planning to dry and store the herb. Just be sure to give plants time to recover before your next harvest.

Fix

Leaves, stems and flowers are all fair game. If thyme stems are pliable, chop them with the leaves and use both as seasoning. (Tougher, drier stems can be saved for soup stocks.)

As a stronger, earthy herb, thyme pairs well with sweet vegetables like squash, onion and potatoes. Season green beans, tarts and even canned fruit for a savory twist, and add it to chutneys, creamy dishes and anything grilled or roasted. It holds its flavor when dried, so if you can't use all your harvest, dry it for later use.

More Perennial Herbs

Anise hyssop. It has a mild anise scent and flavor as well as gorgeous flowers.

Chives. Chives are hardy and easy to grow, and you can eat them from tip to tail (see page 166).

French tarragon. This classic herb flavored with hints of mint and anise is best grown from cuttings.

Lemon verbena. Grown for its fragrance as much as for its culinary appeal, this warm-climate perennial, overwintering down to zone 8, has a fabulous lemon scent.

Lovage. It tastes sort of like celery and grows as tall as 6 feet or more.

Pineapple sage. Rub its leaves between your fingers to take in its pineapple fragrance. It's excellent in teas, baking and beverages and is a hummingbird favorite.

Sorrel. This herb offers a wonderful, tangy flavor to recipes and can be added fresh to green salads.

Rosemary Honey Ice Cream

I love pairing flavors that may seem like an unlikely match but are actually made to be together. This rosemary honey ice cream awakens the senses and changes dessert into something completely new. Use this same method for making other herbed ice creams, from basil and lemon verbena to lavender.

What You Need

1 1/2 cups heavy cream
1 1/2 cups whole milk
1/3 cup honey
1 vanilla bean or 1 tsp. vanilla extract
1 6-inch sprig fresh rosemary (though I often use 2)
4 egg yolks
1 large pinch sea salt

For dairy-free ice cream, substitute full-fat coconut milk for the dairy, or follow the same ratios but use full-fat coconut milk and coconut cream.

What You Do

1. Combine heavy cream, milk, honey, vanilla bean and rosemary sprig in a saucepan. Warm on medium heat, stirring all the while. Remove from heat once bubbles form along the edges of the pan. Cover and let the rosemary sprig steep for 30 minutes.
2. While rosemary is steeping, whisk egg yolks and salt until yolks are light and airy.
3. Remove rosemary sprig and vanilla bean pod from your cream mixture after 30 minutes and return to a gentle simmer. Slowly pour this warmed mixture into the bowl with egg yolks and salt. Whisk until evenly blended and light. This is your custard, or ice cream base.
4. Move the custard back into the saucepan on low to medium heat. Stir continuously until it thickens and forms a coat on the back of a spoon that holds when you run your finger through it. Or test the temperature with an instant-read thermometer. It should register 165 to 170°F (74 to 77°C). As soon as it thickens and reaches this optimal temperature, it can come off the stove.
5. Cover and place in the fridge until cool (may take six to 12 hours).
6. Once the custard is completely cool, transfer it to your ice cream maker and follow the manufacturer's instructions. If you want to be sure all the bits of egg that haven't dissolved in the mix are out, strain the custard through a fine-mesh colander when transferring to your ice cream maker.

Makes about 5 cups.

Summer Fresh Mojito

Mint gives sun tea, salads and tabbouleh new meaning, launching them into the category of bold and refreshing. The same is true for mojitos. What would summer be without a mojito made with mint fresh from the garden?

What You Need

1/2 cup mint simple syrup
3 limes (2 squeezed to yield 1/2 cup juice and
   1 quartered for garnishing)
1 cup rum
1 cup seltzer or soda water (the bubblier the better)
1 bunch spearmint sprigs

What You Do

1. First, make a simple syrup of mint and let it cool.
2. Combine simple syrup, lime juice, rum and soda water in a quart jar or pitcher. Mix well.
3. Serve mojitos in ice-filled glasses with a wedge of lime and a few leaves or a sprig of mint.

SIMPLE SYRUPS

Simple syrups are just that: simple. Combine equal parts sugar and water, warm them until the sugar dissolves, remove from heat, then stir in your favorite herbs or fruits while the mixture is still hot and let them steep. Like tea, the flavors of scented geranium, rosemary or berries infuse into the syrup, and the result is magical.

What You Need

1 part sugar
1 part water
Sprigs or leaves of herbs or fruit

The amount of herbs or fruit you use will depend on the amount of sugar and water. If you start with 1 cup sugar to 1 cup water, you'll need about 5 leaves of herbs, like basil or scented geranium, or 2 or 3 sprigs of rosemary or thyme. If using fruit, use slightly more fruit than syrup combination. Start with 1 1/2 cups fruit to your 1:1 ratio of sugar and water, and experiment until you find the right intensity of flavor.

What You Do

1. Prepare your herbs or fruit.
2. Combine water and sugar in a pot or sauce pan, stir until sugar dissolves and bring to a boil. If you're making a simple syrup with fruit, stir it in at the same time as the sugar.
3. As soon as the mixture boils, remove from heat. Add twigs and leaves for herb infusions. Cover and let steep until the syrup is cool. Once the mixture is cool, run it through a fine-mesh strainer to remove all the bits of plants or fruit, or fish twigs and chunky leaves out with a fork or tongs. Pour your syrup into a clean jar and refrigerate until you're ready to serve.

Serves 4.

TOMATOES
SOLANUM LYCOPERSICUM

Sometimes I grow tomatoes for their fragrance as much as for their fruit. To brush past them in the garden can be as intoxicating as eating them, especially on a warm summer day. In fact, if summer were a fruit, it would be a homegrown tomato. That's reason enough to make room for a tomato plant or two in the garden, or even a set of containers. It also helps that homegrown tomatoes are superior to anything you can buy at the store. With more than 10,000 varieties to choose from, you're bound to find one you'll love.

What You Should Know Before Planting

- Tomatoes come in countless forms and growing habits: some are tall and vining, others are compact; some produce fruit all at once, others continue to fruit through the season.

- Indeterminate varieties are typically vining tomatoes that bear fruit all season and perform well with pruning. They require sturdy cages or staking.

- Determinate varieties are smaller and more compact. They're often referred to as bush tomatoes and are good for smaller spaces, containers and shorter growing seasons. They bear fruit all at once (typically within a one- to two-week period) and don't take pruning, but they do require minimal staking or caging.

- Dwarf tomatoes come in determinate and indeterminate forms. They're incredibly compact, making them ideal for containers, and they often have short growing seasons.

- Vining, or tall, tomatoes can reach up to 6 feet or more if not pruned. Stake or cage them to keep them off the ground and growing with maximum sun exposure. Healthy, productive tomatoes require plenty of rooting space to support the growth flourishing above ground — they're best planted in the ground or in raised beds with 18 inches or more soil depth.

- Bush tomatoes are generally determinate and grow 2 to 5 feet. Grow them in containers or in the ground with cages or stakes, and don't prune them. Some newer hybrids have a longer fruiting time (two to eight weeks).

- Salad tomatoes are sweet, a little tart and juicy. You can enjoy them on the spot in the garden, toss them in salads or serve them as an appetizer.

- Cooking tomatoes generally have low water content and are mild and meaty. Their flavor is fine to bland when eaten fresh but comes to life when cooked or roasted.

- Slicing varieties are a blend of sweet and meaty and are big enough to top a sandwich or burger.

Varieties to Try

'Amish Paste.' This fabulous cooking and eating tomato matures in 85 to 95 days.

'Black Krim.' Many gardeners are happy to wait out an entire summer to enjoy this variety. It's a purply red to brown beefsteak that's perfect for slicing and flavorful enough for salads. Matures in 80 to 90 or more days after transplanting.

'Celebrity.' A compact, high-yielding, disease-resistant determinate plant, it matures in just 65 days.

'Cherokee Purple.' This hefty heirloom is both disease resistant and full of flavor. It grows into a medium-sized vine (4 to 6 feet), is an excellent producer and matures in 80 to 90 days.

'Early Girl' and **'New Girl.'** These are a staple in my garden. If you're working with cool summers or a short growing season, this is a reliable hybrid that matures in just 50 days. Great for eating fresh, slicing or cooking. Their flavor improves with reduced watering while fruit matures.

'Green Zebra.' Gorgeous and sweet with a zing, these tomatoes produce medium-sized fruits, are indeterminate and mature in 75 to 80 days.

Emily's Note

Look for varieties that are disease resistant. Some heirlooms and many hybrids are grown because they have great flavor and are highly disease resistant. Ask your local nursery which diseases to look for, such as fusarium wilt or blight, and which varieties have the best track record for success.

'**Sungold.**' When grown in the right conditions, they pass as candy they're so sweet. This vining hybrid matures in just 55 days and fruits into fall.

'**Yellow Pear.**' A sweet, vining heirloom with small, pear-shaped fruit, this high-yielding salad variety matures in 78 days.

Plant

SUN, MODERATE WATER.

Annual. Prefers rich, well-draining soil. Grow from seed or purchase nursery starts. Easy to germinate. Plant seeds indoors in early spring eight weeks before nighttime temperatures are consistently above 50 to 55°F (10 to 13°C). Cover seeds with 1/4 inch of soil, keep evenly moist and maintain a soil temperature of about 70°F (21°C) for successful germination. Plant out starts as soon as nighttime temperatures are 55°F. Size of plant, spacing and days to maturity depend on variety.

Tomatoes are cold sensitive and need plenty of heat and summer sun to thrive. Unless you live in a region with incredibly hot summers (temperatures consistently above 90°F [32°C] with nighttime temperatures above 75°F [24°C]), give them as much sun and heat as possible. Look for heat-tolerant or cold-tolerant varieties if you're growing on either end of the spectrum.

Harden-off seedlings you've grown from seed before planting them out in the garden to give plants the time they need to acclimate to their new environment. (See page 217 for more information on hardening-off seedlings.) Amend soil with a fresh dose of compost before planting out in the garden, and fertilize once fruit begins to develop. Use a balanced organic fertilizer that contains a source of calcium, like bonemeal or seaweed, and has less nitrogen than phosphorus or potassium (such as a 5-10-4 or a 5-10-10). If you give tomatoes too much nitrogen, plants will make more leaves than fruit. I've also had luck growing tomatoes with no additional amendments other than a side dressing of compost once or twice throughout the growing season. (See page 44 for more on compost and amendments.)

Opposite: Ripen green tomatoes by placing them in a warm spot away from direct sunlight.

WORKSHOP #3

PLANTING AND PRUNING TOMATOES

Before you plant, pinch off the lowest leaves and branches. Roots will grow from these points once buried, which increases root development and creates a stronger, healthier plant. Release your start from its container by squeezing the sidewalls and then tipping it into your hand. Try not to tug at the stem, and if it's root bound, gently tease out the roots.

Move enough soil aside so that your plant will be buried deep enough to cover the new rooting points you made by pinching off leaves and branches. (Ultimately, your start will be half to three-quarters its original height.) Tuck soil in around the plant, pressing near the base of the stem and root zone, making sure it's secure and the roots are making good contact with the soil so it feels anchored and sturdy.

If it's an indeterminate variety, prune your tomato by pinching off the leaves growing from the axillary branching points. True fruiting branches grow out from the plant at a 90-degree angle. The axillary leaves rise at a 45-degree angle and will eventually form into branches with more leaves, taking energy away from flowering and fruiting branches. Pruning also helps keep your plants open and airy, improving circulation and allowing sunlight to do its work. Continue to prune plants as they grow.

Support the plant by staking or caging it. All you need is a single stake, like a long shoot of bamboo, and some twine. Loosely loop the twine around the stem of the tomato and stake, moving the twine up the stake as the plant grows. Finally, once six or so trusses of fruit have formed, pinch off the top of the plant so it stops growing. This will concentrate the plant's energy into a smaller area and, ultimately, produce higher-quality, better-tasting fruit.

Water tomatoes at soil level, and try to keep leaves dry and free of spray. Water consistently, especially if you've planted in containers, and check plants if the weather turns excessively hot. If you're growing tomatoes in the ground or in raised beds with plenty of room for roots to roam, try gradually decreasing waterings the last one-third or so of the plant's life cycle and when fruit is in the final stages of maturing to increase flavor.

Pick

Leave fruit to ripen on the vine as long as possible, harvesting when it easily comes free. Ripe tomatoes are generally fragrant and supple. If you harvest more than you can use, leave them out on the kitchen counter because refrigerated tomatoes lose their flavor.

Pull the last of the fruit off the vine before your first fall frost. Bring unripe fruit inside to ripen indoors, or use in a recipe calling for green tomatoes. To ripen tomatoes indoors, place them in a paper bag out of direct light. If you have a plant loaded with green fruit, pull the entire thing, roots and all. Shake off excess soil and hang it upside down out of direct light and in a warm location.

Fix

Tomatoes are incredibly dynamic. Some lean toward savory, while others are sweet. Sister them with olive oil, the best vinegar you can find, salt and pepper — or nothing at all. The trick is not to overpower the tomato flavor you've worked all these months to foster. Try roasting, or add them to a fresh summer soup. Pair with cheese, basil, marjoram, dill or parsley, and don't forget the garlic.

Slow-Roasted Tomatoes with Fresh Herbs

When tomatoes are at the height of their season and you're craving something new, slow-roasted tomatoes are the answer. The trick is to begin with plum or cooking tomatoes like Romas or another paste tomato, as they tend to be dense and low in water, and their flavor transforms with heat. (Although I must admit, I roast any kind of tomato that's ready to eat.)

What You Need

2 to 4 lb. cooking tomatoes, halved
Olive oil for drizzling
Handful small leaves or chopped, fresh herbs such as thyme, basil, rosemary or parsley
2 or 3 cloves minced garlic *optional
Freshly ground salt and pepper to taste
Red pepper flakes *optional

What You Do

1. Preheat oven to 300°F.
2. Toss tomatoes in a bowl with just enough olive oil to give them a gentle coat. Next, place them in baking pans, open side up.
3. Give each one its own little spot (instead of piling them up as you might with roasted veggies), and sprinkle with 3/4 of your fresh herbs, minced garlic if you're using it, and freshly cracked salt and pepper. Add red pepper flakes now or when serving if you want to spice them up.
4. Place in the oven and roast for 2 hours. Remove from oven and let cool. The longer they're roasted the more flavorful they become. However, if you plan to cook them for multiple hours (4 or more) reduce the heat to 200°F.
5. When they come out of the oven, your tomatoes will look dry on the outside but they'll be wonderfully juicy, sweet and flavorful on the inside. Toss them in salads, pastas or other grain dishes. Pair them with polenta and pesto, or make them into a red sauce or salsa.

Serves 6 to 12.

SUMMER GREENS

LETTUCE, MIZUNA, PURSLANE,
RED LEAF AMARANTH

I used to love watching my grandmother pick and eat leaves in her garden, or even out on walks. Something would catch her eye and she'd take it up with a quick twist and pop it in her mouth. The first time I tried it, I was completely transformed by this simple act. It was liberating in a marvelous, close-to-nature kind of way, and I suddenly saw the plants around me with new eyes. Where I'd once foraged for leafy necklaces, miniature rafts and tiny homes (for who knows what creatures), now I was coveting plants for their texture — and taste.

My fascination with fresh greens hasn't faded, and after years of trial and error, I've finally found a collection of favorites that are reliably delicious and heat tolerant. This is no small feat for leaves in summer — it takes all sorts of adaptations to stay sweet and supple when the sun is beating down and there's fierce competition for water. But this is also what gives this group of greens character and makes each one distinctly delicious.

Lettuce

Lactuca sativa

It's true, greens are easy to grow. But that hasn't stopped me from making mistakes year after year — usually because I lack patience. As much as I'd like to simply chuck some seeds in the ground as I would with radishes or beets, greens like lettuces require a bit more care. Most of the effort comes with selecting the right varieties for the climate, and the rest is in the planting. I find it's best to either direct-sow or, if starting seeds in containers, grow only one seedling per container. Plan to overseed and then thin to one sprout. (This decreases the shock to plants when transplanting because the roots of one plant don't have to be teased apart from the roots of another.)

When choosing which variety to grow, remember lettuce is considered a cool-season crop, preferring the mild temperatures of spring and early fall. It tends to bolt in the heat of summer and fade when temperatures drop in winter. That said, centuries of cultivation have yielded an incredible number of varieties to meet the challenges of gardening in extremes — you don't have to look far to find varieties that are both versatile and delicious.

Varieties to Try

'Batavia.' Just one in a family of summer crisp lettuces that include 'Nevada,' 'Sierra,' 'Tahoe' and 'Rouge Grenobloise,' rugged varieties that grow vigorously regardless of cold and heat.

'Black-Seeded Simpson.' I've had great success with this variety in high-mountain desert climates — it's slow to bolt and is both heat and mildly drought tolerant.

'Flashy Trout Back.' Also known as 'Forellenschluss' and 'Freckles,' this is a heat-tolerant romaine with a delicate, buttery flavor. It's quick to grow and slow to bolt.

'Little Gem.' It's one of the easiest and best-tasting baby romaines out there.

Harvest butter greens leaf by leaf or as head lettuce once it's full and robust.

'Marvel of Four Seasons.' A heat-tolerant butterhead variety that is also remarkably cold tolerant. It develops a cranberry rosette of leaves that are bright green at the base.

'Oak Leaf.' It doesn't tolerate excessive heat but is easy to grow, and its scalloped, oak-shaped leaves can be harvested as a loose-leaf, cut-and-come-again lettuce. Look for both red and green varieties.

'**Red Deer Tongue**' and '**Amish Deer Tongue.**' These flavorful varieties with uniquely triangular leaves are high yielding in both warm summers and cold winters. Harvest as a cut-and-come-again green.

'**Red Sails.**' This fabulous red-leaf lettuce is ready to harvest in just a few weeks. Heat tolerant and slow to bolt, it's best harvested young to use as a baby green.

'**Speckles.**' An Amish heirloom, this butterhead lettuce forms a bib-like head and is both heat tolerant and flavorful.

'**Tom Thumb.**' Another butterhead lettuce, this sweet and mild variety grows well along borders and small containers and is heat tolerant and bolt resistant.

Plant

SUN TO PART SHADE. REGULAR WATER.

Annual. Prefers rich, loose, well-draining soil. Direct-sow seeds, covering with 1/4 inch of soil as soon as soil can be worked, or two to four weeks before the last frost and until two weeks before the first fall frost. Sow in rows or scatter-sow and thin seedlings. For successive crops, sow seeds every three weeks. Get a head start by sowing seeds indoors in trays or paper pots four to six weeks before the last spring frost; transplant out once seedlings are sturdy and about 3 inches tall. Spacing depends on variety. Lettuce seeds germinate when soil temperatures range from 40°F (4°C) to about 80°F (27°C), going dormant when temperatures rise above 85°F (29°C).

Water lettuces regularly and consistently to keep them tender and healthy. Their shallow root systems make them perfect container garden candidates, but it also means the first few inches of soil need to stay damp. Parched lettuces become tough and stunted.

Amend soil with compost before sowing seeds or when planting out seedlings. Apply a light top dressing of manure, compost tea or another organic, nitrogen-rich fertilizer as plants mature. Insulate soil from overheating in the height of summer or from excessive cold in winter by mulching with coarse compost, straw or leaves, which will also help maintain even soil moisture throughout the growing season. (See page 236 for more on feeding your garden.)

You may need to provide plants with shade if growing in a region with intense summer sun. Plant in part shade, provide a shade cover to protect from late afternoon sun, or place plants on the northeast side of taller crops.

Emily's Note

If your seeds aren't germinating or seedlings are wilting at soil level, it could be due to a soil-borne disease called damping-off, which is commonly caused by overly wet and cool soil conditions. (Read more about damping-off, page 214.)

Pick

Lettuces are tender souls that require gentle handling when harvesting to prevent bruising and preserve their vibrant quality. It's best to harvest as needed and treat your pickings carefully. Approach leaf lettuces as cut-and-come-again greens, harvesting leaves from the outside in as plants mature. Gingerly gather outer leaves of head lettuces as they form, leaving the core of the plant intact, and harvest entire heads of lettuce as needed or before weather makes a drastic shift. Use a knife or clippers to cut head lettuce away from the main stem just above soil level.

If lettuce becomes bitter, it's usually a sign that it's bolting or has been exposed to excessive heat. I generally toss it in the compost pile or let it go to seed, then collect and save the seeds to sow.

Fix

Mix and match lettuces with other edible leaves, herbs and ingredients from the garden according to complexity of color, flavor or texture. If you have an especially gorgeous set of leaves, let them stand out on the plate by keeping salads simple. Homegrown salads are the best tasting and don't require heavy dressings — let their flavors shine by matching them with a light vinaigrette. Lettuce can also be braised and sisters well in soups, adding a wonderful, earthy flavor.

Mizuna

Brassica rapa nipposinica or *japonica*

I started growing mizuna when I was working in a school garden and looking for winter veggies that were cold tolerant and would thrive even if largely ignored. What I discovered is a plant that thrives in both winter and summer — and that is impossible to ignore, given its spritely and peppery flavor. Often found in mesclun mixes, mizuna has a hint of bitterness characteristic of mustard greens but is milder and tangier.

Plant

SUN, PART SHADE. MODERATE TO REGULAR WATER.

Biennial grown as an annual. Prefers rich, well-draining soil. Direct-sow from seed, planting 1/4 inch deep. Heat and frost tolerant. Germinates in temperatures as low as 40°F (4°C). Scatter-sow or plant in rows four to six weeks before the last average frost or as soon as soil can be worked in spring. Seed again in summer and fall for winter harvesting. Thin to 4 to 6 inches apart for cut-and-come-again harvesting, or 8 inches if harvesting whole plants. Grows well in containers.

This is a quick-growing plant with lovely, feather-like leaves that are a particularly bright shade of green. Grow with leaf and baby lettuces for your own mesclun mix. A single plant can provide up to two months of harvesting when conditions are right. Sow successively every three to six weeks to optimize the season.

Pick

Begin harvesting outer leaves once plants are 2 inches or taller. Though mizuna is generally slow to bolt in cooler weather, regular harvesting will help prevent plants from shooting up flowers and prolong the harvest period. You can also wait and harvest entire plants when they're more mature.

Fix

Eat it fresh or cooked. Braise with other hardy greens, include in stir-fries (adding it late to cooking so it retains its texture), or serve fresh with a light rice wine vinegar or sesame vinaigrette. Try it with quinoa, in risotto, on a grilled cheese or over pasta. Delicious in miso soup, pickled or fermented.

Purslane

Portulaca oleracea

Weed or edible? It's actually both. Purslane is happy to grow anywhere and has a mild, delicate flavor that's a little citrus-like. It's proficient at self-propagating, and I especially love its succulent nature, which gives it a drought-tolerant edge and a tasty crunch. Its bright green leaves are stunning and uniquely shaped. Tend a patch of wild purslane if you find it in your yard or close by, or grow it yourself from seed.

Plant

SUN. OCCASIONAL TO MODERATE WATER.

Annual. Grows in any soil type, including clay, but most abundant harvests come with worked, well-draining soil. Direct-sow seed without covering or with a light covering — will germinate either way. Scatter-sow or seed in rows, and thin to 6 to 8 inches apart. It's best to keep seeds evenly moist until germinated. Not frost tolerant. Heat tolerant. Performs well even with periods of drought, but grows best with moderate watering. Wild variety is decumbent, trailing along the ground, while the cultivated variety is upright, growing up to 12 inches tall. Grows well in containers.

It's possible to get three or more harvests out of a single sowing, but you may find successive sowings provide the most consistent yields. Plant a fresh batch of seeds every four weeks until six to eight weeks before your first fall frost. While purslane is considered an invasive weed, it's easy to keep under control because its roots are shallow and easily pulled. It grows well in containers and is equally happy in the garden — I've never had trouble with it taking over.

Pick

Gather whole stems of leaves, cutting to the ground, or leave two or three sets of leaves above soil level, cutting just above the uppermost leaf.

Fix

Stems, leaves and flowers are edible. My favorite way to fix them is fresh and tossed in a salad or on a sandwich with cucumber, hummus and fresh tomato. Try adding whole stems with leaves to a stir-fry, a summer veggie soup or pesto.

Red Leaf Amaranth

Amaranthus tricolor

This is a heat-loving, high-yielding plant with stunning foliage. Also known as Chinese spinach, it tastes like a mild kale and can be eaten fresh in salads or cooked like spinach or mustard greens. *Amaranthus viridus* is a similar species worth trying. Both have edible protein-rich seeds that can be cooked like a grain.

Plant

SUN. OCCASIONAL TO MODERATE WATER.

Annual. Prefers well-draining soil of moderate to rich quality. Drought tolerant. Plant from seed; does not transplant well. Sow seeds one to two weeks after your last spring frost, covering with 1/8 to 1/4 inch of soil. Plant three seeds every 6 inches, and thin to one plant per 6 inches. Grows best with summer heat.

If you haven't grown red leaf amaranth, it could soon be your new favorite plant. It's summer hardy, relatively pest free and easy to grow.

Pick

Begin gathering leaves as you need them, starting four weeks after sowing. Harvest continually until it bolts. Plant a fall crop in its place, or let it go to seed. To harvest seeds, simply pull up the entire plant once seeds become dry. Hang it upside down out of the sun and in a warm location. Once entirely dry, place a paper bag over the top of the plant and shake the seeds into the bag.

Fix

Its deep red, streaked leaves stand out in a tossed salad. Try sistering it with other cut-and-come-again greens or in place of kale or spinach. It's perfect with a squeeze of lemon, other summer greens and herbs. Braise or sauté. Add to lasagna, pasta dishes, stir-fries or rice. Pair with cheese and basil or parsley, or use it as a fresh addition to your favorite sandwich.

More Summer Salad Greens

Chicories and endives, *Cichorium intybus* and *C. endivia*. Varieties within these groups grow well in mild summer climates. See Radicchio (page 168) to learn more.

Cilantro, *Coriandrum sativum*. Toss it in a salad or use as a tender herb. (See page 61.)

Malabar spinach, *Basella alba*. Both shade and heat tolerant, Malabar spinach is a climbing vine with edible leaves. Pick leaves as needed, and be careful it doesn't become weedy when growing in mild climates.

Nasturtium, *Tropaeolum spp*. Its leaves are hot and peppery, much like its flowers, adding a welcome punch to a tossed salad. (See page 195.)

'Perpetual Spinach,' *Beta vulgaris*. Not a true spinach but a type of chard, this is a high-yielding, nutritious plant that may become your new favorite edible. (See page 121.)

Swiss chard, *Beta vulgaris*. Grow this incredibly hardy and tenacious variety for a continual supply of greens. (See page 117.)

'Yukina Savoy,' *Brassica rapa*. This is a delicious loose-leaf Chinese cabbage that is quick to mature and easy to grow.

Summer Salad with Meyer Lemon & Chive Vinaigrette

I'm a fan of letting fresh, just-harvested veggies speak for themselves. Why compete with their fabulous, forthright nature by coating them with sticky-sweet, stifling dressings? It's best to stick to complementary, or sometimes contrasting, flavors that heighten the qualities of the individual ingredients, making the finished product downright lovely. Basically, it all comes back to great ingredients. I also think giving greens, whether leafy greens or herbs, a good long soak in cold water adds an extra bit of oomph.

   With this particular dressing, there are no exact amounts because I make dressings in ratios and always make extra for another day or meal.

The ratio of my most basic, everyday dressing is 1/3 vinegar or citrus juice to 2/3 extra-virgin olive oil (the better the olive oil, the better the dressing) combined with freshly ground salt and pepper. Stir or shake and you're done! Adding fresh herbs takes this basic dressing up a level and is the perfect excuse to pick and eat from the garden.

What You Need

Fresh-squeezed Meyer lemon juice (other types of
   lemons are fine, but Meyers tend to be fuller
   and sweeter than Eurekas and others)
Olive oil
Fresh herbs, such as chives, mint, basil, cilantro,
   finely chopped (2 tbsp. for every cup of dressing)
Salt and pepper to taste
1 small garlic clove, finely minced *optional

What You Do

1. Squeeze the lemon(s) into a bowl or jar. Size up how much juice you have, and this is your 1/3.
2. Now add 2/3 olive oil and stir in your fresh herbs and freshly ground salt and pepper; if you're adding garlic, add it now. I find chives and Meyer lemon pair nicely, but so too do lemon and basil. For a tangier twist, lime and cilantro are also fabulous. If you don't have citrus on hand, use vinegar instead.
3. If you're making dressing in a jar, give it a good shake so the salt dissolves and it's ready to serve.

Serving size depends on proportions.

WINTER GREENS

ARUGULA, KALE,
MÂCHE, TATSOI

The rich, peppery leaves of winter greens get their start in summer and early fall. Seeds are sown after temperatures begin to dip and the days become shorter. It may feel strange to make room for them amid ripening tomatoes, abundant basil and a glut of cucumbers, but it's well worth it. Winter greens fill the void left after the final summer harvest and brighten meals with substance that feels all the more meaningful with the changing of seasons.

Arugula

Eruca sativa or E. vesicaria   Diplotaxis tenuifolia

How can so much flavor be packed into such tiny leaves? Arugula is one of my favorite greens. It's a powerhouse that increases in flavor as it matures. I like to scatter-sow seeds, growing them close together to optimize space and simplify harvesting.

Plant

SUN TO SHADE. MODERATE TO REGULAR WATER.

Annual (Erica salvia and E. vesicaria) and perennial (Diplotaxis tenuifolia). Prefers rich, well-draining soil but can grow in lesser soil. Grow from seed or nursery starts. Scatter-sow seeds 1/4 inch deep in cool, moist soil, and thin to about 4 inches apart, eating the thinnings. Plant in late summer once temperatures drop below 75°F (24°C) and again in late winter to early spring as soon as soil can be worked. Best if soil is kept evenly moist. Grows well in containers. Matures in about 35 days. Cold hardy; does not tolerate heat.

This is a quick-growing crop that's easy to sow from seed. Like radishes, there's no need to start arugula in containers unless you're working with limited space and planting successionally. Simply scatter seeds in a prepared bed, press them gently into the soil, then sprinkle a fine layer of compost or planting mix over top, no deeper than 1/4 inch. Water gently, keeping them evenly moist, and they'll be up and growing in a matter of days.

Pick

Harvest individual leaves or whole plants as needed. Leaves tend to become more pungent and spicier as plants go to flower. Gather flowers as they shoot up — they're mild and pretty in a salad — and leave a few to go to seed with the hope of volunteers. Complete harvesting as leaf production declines or when the flavor becomes too strong, and attempt to replant if weather permits.

Fix

Steam or braise the leaves to decrease their kick, or eat them fresh and brighten a salad with their gusto. Pairs well with other hardy greens, such as 'Mizuna,' spinach, 'Perpetual Spinach,' leaf lettuces and mustards. Mellow its flavor by topping it with a hot vinaigrette or pine nuts toasted in olive oil and sprinkled with cheese. Consider combining it with other winter veggies, such as mushrooms, hearty beans or lentils, and root vegetables. I particularly love it with cheeses like chèvre or manchego.

Kale

Brassica oleracea   Brassica napus

My personal rule is to try growing a few new varieties each season. Even so, I keep coming back to 'Red Russian' and 'Lacinato' kale (also known as dino or Tuscan kale). I love 'Red Russian' for its color, frilled edges and texture (it makes a terrific salad of any kind). 'Lacinato' is particularly wonderful when cooked. Its puckered leaves have a mesmerizing way of capturing droplets of water. As it matures, it grows into what looks like small palm trees — like something out of a Dr. Seuss book.

Plant

SUN TO LIGHT SHADE. MODERATE TO REGULAR WATER.

Biennial grown as an annual. Prefers rich, well-draining soil. Grow from seed or starts. Sow seeds in midsummer to fall and again in winter for a spring harvest, planting 1/2 inch deep. Spacing depends on variety and harvesting. Grows well in containers but requires more planting depth than mizuna and arugula.

I find birds enjoy kale sprouts as much as I do. When direct-sowing in the garden, consider covering seedlings with netting to protect them until they're big enough to fend for themselves. Siberian kale doesn't transplant well and is best sown in place, but many other varieties can be started indoors and transplanted out or purchased as nursery starts.

Like so many winter vegetables, kale becomes sweeter as temperatures drop. It's hardy, tolerating temperatures down to 20°F (-7°C), and it's also likely to bolt and become infested with aphids as temperatures rise in summer. My kale comes out around May or June and finds its way back into the garden in September and October.

Pick

Harvest and eat kale at any point, removing outer leaves where the leaf stem meets the main stem. It's tasty as a microgreen and, if left to mature, can provide weeks, even months, of harvesting.

Fix

Trim stems and eat kale raw in salads, as a coleslaw or in a tabouleh with quinoa. Try adding it to stir-fries or pairing it with white beans and garlic topped with chèvre on pasta. Add it to soups, enchiladas, grain dishes or pesto. It holds its own in an incredible range of dishes, making it all the more worthwhile to grow your own.

Emily's Note

Kale and its brassica relatives are host plants for cabbage white butterflies. If you start seeing large holes or entire leaves missing, it's probably the butterfly larvae (aka cabbage worms). They're small, bright green and smooth. Pick them off in the mornings and evenings, or spray plants with OMRI-certified organic Bt (Bacillus thuringiensis, a naturally occurring soil-borne bacteria). Read more about tackling pests on page 251.

Mâche

Valerianella locusta

Once considered a weed, mâche is having a moment. A delicacy rarely found in markets, you'll need to sow it yourself to appreciate its full flavor and capabilities. While tender and sweet, mâche can also hold its own against a variety of flavors, although I also love it by itself in a simple salad. It may take 60 days or longer to harvest and grow within a small window of the year, but this is also what makes it exceptional, like a limited edition.

Plant

SUN TO LIGHT SHADE. OCCASIONAL TO MODERATE WATER.

Annual. Prefers rich, well-draining soil. Sow from seed, planting 1/4 to 1/2 inch deep from August through fall. Plant three seeds every 4 inches and thin to 4-inch spacing, or scatter-sow for a green manure. Germinates best when temperatures are between 50 and 65°F (10 to 18 °C). Slow to grow, matures in 60 days. Hardy. Needs straw mulch or other cover when temperatures drop below 5°F (-15°C).

While you'll need to start mâche from seed, it's also happy to volunteer and can become established in your garden with little help once it gets going. Look for seeds at your nursery or in a seed catalog. It's also known as corn salad or lamb's lettuce.

Pick

Harvest outer leaves as plants mature or whole plants, cutting just below the soil surface. Use a small, sharp knife or precision clippers to help with gathering. Leave a handful of plants to go to flower and set seed. Once they're established, these self-sowers will do the work of planting for you.

Fix

I love letting the flavor of the greens shine through, especially when their character is easily drowned out when overdressed. Try preparing mâche with a light dressing of fresh-squeezed lemon and olive or walnut oil (my favorite). In Europe, it's often served with bacon or with mushrooms. Sauté chanterelles and toss with mâche before serving with a squeeze of lemon and a pinch of salt. It also pairs well with roasted beets, eggs and fish.

Tatsoi

Brassica rapa var. narinosa

Have you ever wondered about those cute, spoon-like leaves in your mesclun mix? They're probably tatsoi, an eager-to-grow mustard. With just 45 days to maturity, this is a perfect plant for small gardens and containers. It's high yielding, nutritious and flavorful.

Plant

FULL TO PART SUN. MODERATE TO REGULAR WATER.

Annual. Prefers rich, well-draining soil. Direct-sow or start indoors and transplant out from spring through fall. Bury seeds 1/4 to 1/2 inch deep, and space 6 to 8 inches apart, or sow thickly for baby greens. Incredibly cold hardy; cover to protect from winter weather, and harvest through the season, even from under a blanket of snow.

Tatsoi is quick to germinate and mature. Amend soil with compost, manure or worm tea to grow an abundant supply of leafy greens. While it can be grown in summer, its flavor comes to life with the cool temperatures of fall and winter.

If you're not sure what to grow, try scatter-sowing mâche (opposite) or tatsoi (above) as an edible cover crop.

Pick

Harvest individual leaves by pinching them off or bending them at a right angle near the leaf base. Shear patches of leaves for baby greens. If growing heads, gather outer leaves first, and cut just above soil level when harvesting entire heads.

Fix

Delicious raw or lightly cooked. Add to salads or to a stir-fry just as it comes off the heat, or toss into a soup at the last minute. Use it in place of spinach, lettuce or other Asian greens.

More Winter Salad Greens

Chicories and endives, *Cichorium intybus* and *C. endivia*. Start in summer and fall for a winter harvest. (See Radicchio, page 168.)

'Komatsuna,' *Brassica rapa* var. *perviridis*. Also known as Japanese mustard spinach, this high-yielding green can be eaten much like mustards and 'mizuna.'

Miner's lettuce, *Claytonia perfoliata*. A charming plant, native to parts of the western United States. It's a terrific self-seeder, likes part shade and is succulent and mellow. Best grown in mild climates or under shelter.

'Mizuna,' *Brassica rapa nipposinica*. Both heat tolerant and cold hardy, it can be grown year-round in many climates.

Mustard greens, *Brassica juncea*. The size and dramatic colors of 'Red Giant' and 'Garnet Giant' are gorgeous in winter gardens, plus they're wonderful to eat. (Smaller varieties, like 'Ruby Streaks,' will help optimize space.)

'Pak choy,' *Brassica rapa* var. *chinensis*. Try this Chinese cabbage sautéed lightly with sesame oil.

Spinach, *Spinacia oleracea*. A member of the amaranth family, it's best sown in fall for a winter and spring harvest.

Savory Galette

Main course, side dish, appetizer or dessert — this savory galette is all of those things wrapped up in a fabulous crust. Your favorite crust, as a matter of fact. It's a win-win. Just make it once and you'll find it's easy to substitute one veg or green for another, and it turns out wonderfully every time. I must qualify this recipe as a "no recipe" recipe. (My husband would say: "Is this another Emily creation?") Honestly, it's a crave-driven affair, where whatever sounds good in a given moment plays the leading role. Toss wilted greens, fresh herbs, nuts, capers and cheese into a pastry, and bake it to perfection.

What You Need

THE FILLING

A pile of greens, which amounts to about two big handfuls or bunches of greens suitable for cooking. I'm a fan of dino kale, but mustard greens, chard and perpetual spinach also work well.

I always include:
2 or 3 spring onions, depending on size
A couple cloves of garlic
Olive oil
Salt and pepper to taste
Nuts, such as pine nuts
Cheese, like Parmesan
Fresh herbs
Mustard or another spread

Other filling possibilities:
Mushrooms, sweet or spicy peppers, beets, leeks, roasted squash, potatoes, Jerusalem artichokes, shaved fennel bulb, celeriac, olives, capers

THE CRUST

Ingredients for your favorite pie or pastry crust with plans to spice it up. Start with a basic recipe; one with a combination of white and wheat flour, salt, butter and ice-cold water works well. Consider adding flavors that heighten heartiness, like finely grated Parmesan, black pepper or even a little jalapeno. It's also possible to substitute apple cider vinegar for some of the water, or skip the gluten and make a crust with corn meal or gluten-free flour. Plus, you'll need a mixture of egg whites and milk to coat the crust and give it a glaze at the end before it goes into the oven.

What You Do

1. First, make your filling. I start by prepping my greens, de-ribbing dense stems (like kale stems) and chopping them coarsely before putting them into a bowl of cool water to wash and hydrate them before running them through a salad spinner. Then, I chop some onion and garlic, sauté it in olive oil until it's nearly translucent, and add the greens with a little salt, pepper and even some red pepper flakes. If including mushrooms and other veggies with high moisture content, add them to the onions and garlic to sauté before adding greens.

2. Once the greens wilt and turn a bright shade of green, take them off the stove. If they're really juicy, drain off the excess moisture. (Watery greens make for a watery galette.)

3. Preheat your oven to 400°F.

4. Mix greens and other filling ingredients in a bowl. Taste it for flavor, and add spices or herbs accordingly. Then, set it aside while you make your crust. (I make the crust second so it's cold and easy to work.)

5. Roll the crust out so it forms a basic circle that's about 10 inches in diameter and thick enough to fold without falling apart. Place it on a baking sheet lined with parchment.

6. Spread a thin layer of something savory like Parmesan cheese, mustard or pepper jam over the crust as a buffer between the crust and the filling. Pile your filling on top. Spread it evenly, but leave room along the edges to fold your galette. (Two inches should be plenty.)

7. Fold the borders in sections to make the most pleasing shape possible. Hexagons work well, but mine always look a little hodge-podgy. For the glaze, whip one egg white with milk or cream and paint it on your crust with a basting brush.

8. Sprinkle it with cheese and fresh herbs, and pop it in the oven.

9. Bake for 30 minutes or until golden brown and flaky. Cover with foil if your sprinkling of cheese is cooking faster than your crust.

10. Serve warm right away with salad, or eat it all by itself. (Or all by yourself!)

Serves 6.

HARDY GREENS

CHARD & PERPETUAL SPINACH

These stalwart greens bridge the seasons, providing months of harvesting with little care. Plant once in early spring and harvest until temperatures drop at the beginning of winter — you may even find you're able to harvest throughout the winter and into the following spring if you live in a milder climate.

Chard and perpetual spinach are both of the same species, *Beta vulgaris*. They're leafy beets that don't grow a fleshy, edible root but instead put their energy solely into producing greens.

Chard or Swiss chard

Beta vulgaris (Cicla Group)

I once found chard volunteering in a school garden greenhouse. It had taken root in an unlikely spot of gravel, and I couldn't bring myself to harvest its leaves. Chard is both versatile and dashing. Plant it along borders where it can't be missed or in large swaths for visual impact. Grow combinations of 'Peppermint Stick' or 'Bright Lights' for color, or 'Fordhook Giant' for its enduring nature and stately leaves. Look for cut-and-come-again varieties of baby leaf chard that can be planted and harvested by shearing (like a haircut). It's a welcome friend in any garden, growing well in containers or beds that have plenty of rooting depth — 12 inches or more should do.

Because chard leaves are lovely

Plant

SUN TO PART SHADE. REGULAR WATER.

Biennial. Prefers rich soil with excellent drainage. Direct-sow seeds two to three weeks before your last spring frost, or start indoors about four weeks before your last spring frost. Bury seeds 1/2 inch deep. Transplant seedlings to the garden when they've grown true leaves and they're about four weeks old. Sow until eight weeks before your first fall frost. Thin seedlings to 10 to 12 inches apart, leaving the sturdiest sprouts. Apply organic compost tea later in summer to give them a boost. Mulch planting beds well and provide protection when temperatures dip below 15°F (-9.4°C).

Proper spacing between plants improves air circulation and decreases diseases common to chard. A layer of mulch applied to planting beds helps with this too, decreasing splashing and therefore the likelihood of transmitting fungi from soil to leaves.

Water consistently for the best-tasting and most bolt-resistant chard, and provide shade in extreme heat or as protection from intense sun. Consider planting on the north side of taller crops when growing chard in regions with hot summers.

If you have room to spare, don't give up on chard after the first frost. Instead, mulch it well and you may be surprised by a spring crop of greens.

Emily's Note

Chard seeds are actually tiny dried fruits that contain two or three seeds, which is why you may find three plants sprouting where you planted only one seed.

Pick

Harvest leaves at any size, picking from the outside in. Gather a handful of leaves per plant at any one time, but leave enough for plants to continue growing through the seasons. Gather leaves as needed or rinse and store in the refrigerator for up to three days.

Fix

Eat smaller, tender leaves fresh in salads or cook as you would spinach. Chop leaves and stalks, using both in any given recipe, or use separately. Try adding them to soups, pastas, pizza and calzones. Risotto, grain salads, quiche and empanadas also benefit from the addition of chard. Use leaves as wraps, stuffing as you would manicotti and topping with a light layer of marinara. Stalks can be grilled or braised like asparagus.

Perpetual Spinach

Beta vulgaris (Cicla Group)

Perpetual spinach has the flavor and tenderness of spinach, but with the hardiness of chard. When in full swing, it's prolific, producing fabulous yields of greens even through the heat of summer. (When true spinach has already gone to seed.) It's a tasty, adaptable one-stop shop. Plant in spring and reap the benefits for months without successional seeding.

Plant

SUN TO PART SHADE. REGULAR WATER.

Biennial. Prefers rich soil with excellent drainage. It's best to direct-sow seeds two to three weeks before your last spring frost and sow again in late summer, eight weeks before your first fall frost. Thin seedlings to about 8 inches apart, leaving the sturdiest sprouts. Apply organic, compost tea in summer to give them a boost. Mulch planting beds well and provide protection when temperatures dip below 15°F (-9.4°C).

Get more from leafy greens like perpetual spinach (above) and other chards (opposite) with continual harvesting.

Once sown, the goal is to keep soil evenly moist to prevent stress and possible bolting when temperatures rise in midsummer. Like chard, it can be grown in part shade or on the north side of taller crops to give it a break from the summer sun.

Perpetual spinach will continue growing and producing greens throughout winter and early spring in mild climates. In colder winter climates, it's possible to over winter perpetual spinach with mulching and a cold frame for a repeat of greens in spring along with seed setting.

Pick

Leaf stems are thinner than chard, making it easy to twist or cut them free from plants. Pick the outside leaves first, leaving inside leaves to continue cropping.

Fix

The leaves of perpetual spinach are tender enough to be tossed in salads and used as you would true spinach. It's fabulous when paired with fresh-squeezed lemon, garlic and feta or chèvre. Add it to quiche, spanakopita, pizza, pastas and quinoa or other grain salads. Toss it in your juicer; sister it with summer herbs and tomatoes; add it to pesto or a garden-fresh soup.

Varieties to Try

'**Baby Leaf.**' This cut-and-come-again variety is designed to be sown and harvested as a thick carpet. Grows well in containers.

'**Fordhook Giant.**' Another mild-flavored chard, it is also one of the hardiest.

'**Italian Silver Rib.**' An heirloom classic and favorite of Italian cooks, this chard is crunchy and mellow.

'**Pot of Gold.**' It has bright gold stems and grows well in containers.

'**Rainbow Chard**' and '**Bright Lights.**' These seed combinations produce colorful beds of chard, with stems ranging from gold to pink. They're gorgeous in the garden, but not as cold hardy as varieties with white and cream-colored stems.

'**Scarlet Charlotte.**' This chard is characterized by deep-red stems and leaf veins and green, crinkly leaves.

'**Vulcan Chard.**' This variety is incredibly heat tolerant and prolific.

Favorite Frittata

If you find you have more greens than you know what to do with, or you're looking for breakfast for dinner or the perfect complement to salad and soup, this is it. It's so yummy and easy to make, I've been tempted to eat it all myself in one go.

I usually let chard dominate, but herbs like cilantro or basil can easily be substituted one for another. Parsley also pairs well with fresh thyme, and it's possible to include tender greens like perpetual spinach, mizuna and tatsoi or other mustards.

Serves 4 to 6.

What You Need

1 lb. chard or a combination of other greens like mizuna, tatsoi, perpetual spinach
1 cup spring onions, diced
2 to 4 cloves garlic, depending on size and preference
Splash of olive oil
2 whole eggs
6 egg whites
1/2 cup grated Parmigiano Reggiano
4 tbsp. chopped tender herbs such as basil, cilantro, thyme, sorrel, and parsley
Salt and pepper to taste (I usually add about 1/4 tsp. each)

What to Do

1. Preheat oven to 375°F.
2. Chop and wash greens. If using Swiss chard, remove the larger, tougher stems and coarsely chop. Soak greens in cold water while you prep and sauté the onions and garlic with a dash of olive oil for about 3 minutes in a large skillet or until they become tender.
3. Add greens and cover, stirring occasionally for about 10 minutes or until greens turn bright green. Remove from heat, and pour off excess liquid if necessary.
4. Whip eggs and egg whites in a large bowl until frothy. Mix in cheese, herbs, and salt and pepper, stirring for 1 to 2 more minutes. (I'm convinced the extra stirring enlivens the dish, giving it a loftier consistency.) Fold in greens.
5. Coat an 8-inch cast iron skillet with olive oil and heat in the oven until warm. Pour mixture into warm skillet and return to the oven for about 12 minutes. You'll know your frittata is cooked through when it's just beginning to brown and a knife comes out clean from the center.
6. Serve immediately. It's perfect as breakfast, lunch or dinner with a fresh salad and seasonal veggies.

ROOT VEGETABLES

BEETS, CARROTS, ONIONS, RADISHES, TURNIPS

It wasn't until I moved from the coast of northern California to the Sierra Nevada Mountains that I discovered the sweetness of winter firsthand. Weather is mild along the coast, whereas in the mountains temperatures dip well below zero in winter and can hover just above freezing on summer nights, following a daytime high of 85°F (29°C). This presents a few gardening challenges, but frigid temperatures also come with benefits.

Like the heat of summer, cold has a way of defining sugars and heightening flavor. In winter, the response of converting starches to sugar is designed to protect plants from freezing and is what takes vegetables like carrots to a whole new level of amazing. Grow winter veggies (greens included) through a cold spell or over-winter veggies planted in fall for a spring harvest, and the result is transformative.

Beets
Beta vulgaris

Beets range from earthy to sweet, and with so many varieties to choose from, I find I need to be strategic in my planting and choose varieties that have the biggest impact. I tend to weigh which of these versatile veggies I can plant that will both augment daily meals and grow into something uniquely wonderful that can be juiced, roasted or pickled.

Plant

SUN TO LIGHT SHADE. OCCASIONAL TO MODERATE WATER.

Biennial grown as an annual. Prefers light, well-draining soil. Scatter-sow or plant in rows or triangles, planting 1/2 inch deep, and thin to 3 or 4 inches, depending on the varieties and your harvesting preferences. Cold hardy. Begin sowing seeds four weeks before the last frost until temperatures rise to 75°F (24°C). Sow again as weather cools, about two months before the first frost.

Direct-sow seeds or transplant when young, and consider presoaking seeds to speed up germination (see page 216). They can take some shade but perform best in full sun. They're also somewhat drought tolerant, although I've found it's best not to skimp too much on watering as it can stunt their growth, making their roots stringy and fibrous.

Pick

Harvest when roots are young and tender for the best flavor — about 1 inch in diameter for baby beets or 2 inches in diameter when mature. It's possible to pick leaves while roots are developing, though sparingly.

Fix

The sweetness of beets pairs well with the acids of lemon and vinegar. Tangy yogurts also complement beets nicely, balancing the richness of their flavor, whether sweet or earthy. Pickle, ferment or roast. Add them to salads with goat cheese, pickled onion and greens like arugula or mâche. You can also toss them into curry for an unexpected twist or dice them into risotto.

Varieties to Try

'Chioggia.' On the earthy end of the spectrum, they produce fabulous candy-striped roots.

'Detroit Dark Red.' This heirloom is on the sweet end of the spectrum.

'Early Wonder.' This variety grows best in cool soil and produces a wonderful crop of greens.

'Golden.' These reliable producers are sweet and rich in flavor.

Carrots

Daucus carota subsp. sativus

Growing carrots can be tricky. It can take a few seasons to get to know their ways and devise a surefire method for guaranteed harvests — it can be heartbreaking when they don't come up as planned. But it's worth it to keep trying. I've found that the times I take less notice, scattering them in among flowers and other plants, is when they do best.

Plant

SUN. REGULAR WATER.

Biennial grown as an annual. Requires light, sandy soil that's free of obstacles. Direct-sow in spring once the chance of frost is past and until two months before the first fall frost. Sow gingerly to decrease thinning, planting 1/4 inch deep. Seeds are tiny, so mix them with sand to help separate them, making them easier to handle. Thin to about 3 inches apart. Maintain even soil moisture, especially during the germination process. Germinates best in warm soils, about 75°F (24°C), but with a range of 50 to 85°F (10 to 29°C). Slow to grow, taking 70 days or more to mature.

Emily's Note

Carrots are slow to germinate and picky about soil moisture and temperature. Sow seeds when temperatures are at the warm end of their optimal range (75°F [24°C] is ideal). Maintain even soil moisture throughout germination. I've found that covering carrot seeds with a light layer of vermiculite instead of soil helps maintain even soil moisture right at seed level, increasing your odds of success.

Grow carrots in a planter filled with sandy soil, or in a raised bed with light, well-conditioned loose soil. Avoid soils recently amended with manures or other dense fertilizers. I like to tuck them in with tomatoes, radishes and companion plants like nasturtium and marigolds. Carrots are highly susceptible to a pest aptly called carrot fly, which finds its host through scent when flying low to the ground. The fragrances of companion plants help mask the scent of carrots.

Choose varieties best suited to your planting area. Look for short, stubby varieties like 'Little Finger' carrots for shallow containers and 'Scarlet Nantes' or a rainbow blend when working with planters with deeper rooting areas.

Pick

Immature carrots don't have the same concentration of flavors as older carrots. Use the "days to maturity" information on your seed packet as a guideline. You can let them sit in the soil past this period, but wait too long and they become fibrous. (Or use the good old-fashioned way of harvesting: push the soil away from the crown, and if the carrot looks good, eat it.)

Fix

Juice, cook or eat carrots raw and straight from the garden. Try them steamed, braised or roasted with fresh herbs. They sister well with chervil, parsley, ginger, dill or, really, whatever is fresh from the garden.

Onions

Allium cepa

I can't imagine a garden without onions. They're fabulous companion plants and tuck in neatly between other crops, providing a visual display of spiky greens. You can harvest them as needed, leaving the rest in the ground for another meal or until cool weather sets in.

Plant

SUN. MODERATE TO REGULAR WATER.

Annual. Prefers rich, well-draining soil. It's possible to direct-sow seeds, starting them as soon as soil can be worked, although this requires patience. Grow them from sets for more immediate results and sure harvests. To grow from sets, plant an inch deep with roots pointing down, about 3 to 4 inches apart, depending on the desired size of bulb at harvest. Plant in early spring and successively into fall in mild climates.

　　Onion sets come in assorted varieties. Look for a mix of red, white and yellow for fun and flavor. They tend to not grow as large as onions planted from seed, but the flavor is excellent and the return on effort phenomenal. Tuck them into your garden wherever there is a spot, or line edges of beds with them to deter pests. Shallots can be grown much the same way.

Pick

Harvest onions at any point in their development. The smaller they are, the more tender. Use them as green onions, or pick as spring onions when the bulb has just begun to develop, and leave others in the ground to continue growing.

Fix

Chop, dice or thinly slice. Roast or sauté with other veggies. Add to soups, salads, sauces and other savory dishes — I put them in pretty much everything.

Radishes

Raphanus sativus

Radishes are incredibly reliable and quick to grow, maturing in just a matter of weeks. Chuck some seeds in the ground and see what happens. Radishes germinate in just three to seven days, and the near immediate results of watching them sprout and take root is exciting!

Plant

SUN TO LIGHT SHADE. MODERATE TO REGULAR WATER.

Annual. Prefers rich, well-worked soil but will grow in poor soils. Direct-sow, planting 1/2 inch deep and thinning to about 2 inches apart. Sow as soon as soils can be worked in spring, and continue planting until the first frost. Germinates in 40°F (4°C) soil but does best when soil temperatures range from 60 to 65°F (16 to 18°C).

Plant radishes little and often for successive harvesting. This also makes the job of thinning easier. I find the extra time I take to provide each individual seed space when sowing pays off in the long run, saving time later. However, I always end up thinning a few to prevent overcrowding and then add the thinnings to salads or sandwiches.

I find tried-and-true varieties like 'Cherry Belles' and 'French Breakfast' rewarding, but it's also fun to grow 'Watermelon' radishes or the impressive 'Candela Di Fuoco,' which are long and tapered like carrots.

Pick

Begin harvesting in three to four weeks. You'll find the radishes that had the most sun with plenty of water and good soil quality mature the fastest, so look to these first and let any stragglers catch up.

Fix

We generally approach radishes as a snack, something to eat in ones and twos, as an appetizer or chopped into a salad. Cooking them mellows their flavor, but it's still present. They're also wonderful roasted with other winter vegetables. Try them with lemon or lime, cilantro or parsley, served over rice or in a grain salad. I especially love them with potatoes and a little dill and served over rice or in a grain salad.

Turnips

Brassica rapa

For many of us, turnips are a learn-to-love vegetable. Some say this is because they have long been known as fodder for livestock and grown into large, thick-skinned roots with little appeal. I was first introduced to the possibilities of turnips through my CSA share based in the foothills of California (USDA hardiness zone 8). It helped that the farm also sent recipe suggestions along with the first batch of gorgeous, buttery white 'Tokyo Market' turnips with bright green leaves still attached.

Plant

SUN. REGULAR WATER.

Biennial grown as an annual. Prefers rich, loose soil. Direct-sow, planting 1/2 inch deep and thinning to about 2 to 4 inches apart, depending on variety. Cold hardy. Protect sprouts from birds with row cover or netting.

Quick to grow, with most varieties maturing in 30 to 50 days. Keep them well watered during the germination process (five to 10 days), and weed as needed. Sow little and often to minimize thinning and to ensure a continuous crop.

Pick

Thin seedlings to prevent crowding, and eat them as you go. Gather turnips when they're as small as 1 inch in diameter, or let them grow for a more substantial harvest.

Fix

Turnips are tender and can be eaten raw when picked young or slightly smaller than their expected full maturity size. Toss them in a salad or eat them as you would a radish or carrot. When cooking, leave them in the ground until you're ready to add them to a recipe. This ensures the greens will be fresh. I generally use the roots and the greens together, even if a recipe doesn't call for both. (The pungency of the greens marries well with the sweetness of the roots.)

Try making a turnip soup with greens and whole-grain bread. Roast or braise sliced turnips in a little olive oil, and toss the greens in at the end. The greens are also wonderful wilted in a sprinkle of water with a dash of salt. Cook them until they turn a brighter shade of green but still hold their integrity as a leaf. You can also grate turnip with apple, toss with parsley and add olive oil and vinegar for a quick slaw.

The leaves of many root vegetables, including turnips (above), beets, onions, radishes and even carrots, are edible and nutritious.

Varieties to Try

'**Mikado.**' Also called Japanese baby turnips, they're pearly white and delicious. They're also some of the quickest to mature and have greens that are just as tasty as the roots.

Tokyo market turnips

'**Purple Top White Globe.**' This standard garden variety is productive, easy to grow and flavorful.

'**Scarlet Queen.**' Its white flesh and spicy red skin is tasty when cooked or enjoyed raw in salads.

'**Seven Top.**' These are a wonderful option thanks to their masses of nutritious greens.

'**Tokyo Market**' and '**Hakurei.**' Similar to 'Mikado,' they germinate and mature quickly and have fabulous flavor.

Roasted Root Vegetables with Citrus, Herbs, Chilies & Pomegranate

I find the simplest recipes are often the most jaw-dropping, especially when made with the freshest ingredients. It's not necessary to overdress roasted vegetables — they're far better underdressed as then you can taste each and every nuance. My usual go-to recipe is to toss them in the best olive oil I can find with salt and pepper. Sometimes I add fresh herbs, citrus and pomegranate and occasionally chili peppers.

What You Need

1 lb. or more carrots, sliced longways from tip to tail
1 lb. or more beets, quartered
Handful turnips or radishes or both *optional
2 or more onions, cut in rounds or quartered so they fall apart in flakes
1 blood orange, cut into rounds
Fresh herbs such as dill, basil, thyme, rosemary, marjoram, parsley*
1/2 pomegranate, seeded
2 bay leaves
2 chili peppers, whole
Cinnamon stick *optional
Salt and pepper to taste
Extra-virgin olive oil

*Note: I like to coarsely chop herbs like thyme and marjoram.

What You Do

1. Preheat oven to 350°F.
2. Wash and chop vegetables, slice the orange into rounds, and prepare herbs and pome-granate. Toss vegetables, orange, bay leaves, chili peppers, cinnamon (if using), salt and pepper, and perennial herbs in a bowl or on a baking sheet, and coat with olive oil until glistening.
3. Bake about 45 to 60 minutes. Remove from oven once vegetables are soft and beginning to brown and caramelize.
4. Sprinkle with pomegranate seeds and fresh, tender herbs like dill before serving.

Serves 6 to 8.

Cucumbers & Summer Squash

Lemon cucumbers were a staple in my paternal grandfather's garden. He was a dear man of Portuguese descent with a farm in Sonoma, California, where he kept dairy cattle, had a pear orchard and grew rows of carrots in winter, cucumbers in summer. The rough, heart-shaped leaves of lemon cucumbers would sprawl down mounds he shaped when planting. They grew like mad during the hottest days of summer, producing little yellow flowers and round, lemon-like fruits. We ate them straight from the garden, picking around their prickly skins.

It's hard to imagine a summer garden without cucumbers, or squash for that matter. They speak of heat and sun and earthy goodness. They can produce without end, yielding a regular supply of fruit for months when the growing is good — and you don't need a farm to grow them. They're happy to climb an A-frame trellis or lean out and trail between beds, offering lettuces and other shade-loving plants protection from the heat of the day.

Cucumbers

Cucumis sativus

Grow 'Persian' cucumbers for their small, finger-like fruits, cucumbers for pickling, or English cucumbers for slicing. As with so many other edibles, I prefer varieties with fabulous flavor, as well as ones I have trouble finding at the store. (I always grow lemon cucumbers because they tether me to my family.)

There are some cucumber-like fruits that aren't true cucumbers. One is the Armenian cucumber, *Cucumis melo* var. *flexuosus*. It looks and tastes like a cucumber but is technically a melon. Another is a tiny, watermelon-like fruit with more than one common name: cucamelon, mouse melon and Mexican sour gherkin are just a few. (Thank goodness for its scientific name, *Melothria scabra,* or imagine the confusion.) It's adorable, crunchy and excellent raw or pickled. It's also hardier than true cucumbers, growing into fall even as temperatures drop.

Plant

SUN. MODERATE TO REGULAR WATER.

Annual. Prefers rich, well-draining soil. Direct-sow two weeks after the last spring frost, or start indoors two to four weeks before the last spring frost and transplant out once weather is warm and seedlings have two true leaves. Bury seeds 1/2 to 1 inch deep, depending on

variety, and space 18 inches apart or more, depending on variety. Keep soil evenly moist and warm (65°C/18°F or warmer) through germination for best results.

Mounding or hilling soil before seeding or transplanting is a helpful trick for preventing plant roots from becoming waterlogged. Since water runs downhill, any excess water from an unexpected downpour or accidental overwatering will move away from the root zone, which is particularly important for cucumbers. While they thrive with consistent watering, they can also suffer from root rot when sitting in water. (See page 230 for watering tips.)

On the other hand, cucumbers grown without enough water can become bitter. The trick is to give plants just enough water to start combined with well-worked, healthy soil that's high in organic matter, then to water deeply and consistently as they grow.

Emily's Note

Trellis vining cucumbers to save space, improve air circulation, produce straighter fruit and make harvesting easier.

Pick

For the best-tasting cucumbers, harvest as frequently as possible when fruits are smaller in size. (This will also stimulate further flowering and fruit production.) Fruit left on the vine to overmature will signal to the plant that it's time to begin wrapping up its life cycle, which slows fruit production.

When harvesting, it's best to cut or pinch fruit off the vine where the stem and fruit meet instead of pulling. Store cucumbers at room temperature, not in the fridge. Cucumbers can become damaged from the cold and are also more likely to get wet and deteriorate more quickly. Instead, make sure they're dry and set them out on your kitchen counter, but away from bananas or tomatoes for the longest storage. (Bananas and tomatoes produce ethylene gas, which speeds ripening.)

Finding treasure in the garden

Fix

Some cucumbers are grown for pickling, while others are grown for eating fresh, and still others are excellent for both. Eat them plain, on sandwiches, in salads or as a garnish. Make tzatziki by squeezing cucumbers and mixing the pulp with Greek yogurt, garlic, lemon juice and dill. Pickle or ferment them with dill and other summer herbs.

Cucamelons are also excellent pickled. However, eat the teeny ones fresh, when they're most tender, and pickle the larger ones when they're about an inch in length. I find they're best when pickled in a hot-water bath after being sliced in half.

Varieties to Try

Armenian cucumber. Excellent for slicing and mild in flavor, they're best harvested when they're 12 to 18 inches long.

'Beit Alpha.' Delicious, uniform in size and perfect for pickling and eating fresh, this cucumber is sweet and versatile.

'Boston.' Crisp and flavorful, this classic pickling cucumber is an heirloom from the 1800s.

Grow summer squash (opposite) not only for its fruit but also for its edible flowers and fabulous, playful leaves.

'Crystal Apple.' Creamy white with an apple shape, it's also prolific, mild in flavor and best when eaten fresh.

'Lemon.' Wonderful for eating fresh, they're also fairly disease resistant, are highly productive and tolerate low water conditions without becoming bitter.

'Persian.' Crunchy and never bitter, these are best when harvested at four to six inches long.

'Spacemaster.' A slicing cucumber, it's ideal for small gardens or large containers.

'Tasty Jade.' This burpless Japanese cucumber is a reliable producer, grows quite long and is excellent for slicing and eating fresh.

Summer Squash
Cucurbita pepo

The biggest problem with summer squash is finding a way to eat them all. There is always a period of time in summer when I scour recipe books looking for new ways to cook, grill or bake my way through their numbers. Best of all, their flowers are gorgeous and edible, they make fabulous companion plants and they're water-wise.

The yellow and orange glow of squash blossoms are like bright lights in the garden, drawing bumblebees, insects of all kinds — and us. They're a fleeting delicacy, with zucchini and pumpkins producing some of the most flavorful, though the blossoms of all summer and winter squash are edible.

Place squash near the base of green beans or along borders where they can fill in gaps or cover untended areas. Their trailing vines with large, bristly leaves act as a living mulch, insulating the soil and decreasing water loss from the surface. These same bristly hairs also help regulate temperature and transpiration for the individual plants. The shading the leaves provide even helps prevent weed growth.

Plant

SUN. MODERATE TO REGULAR WATER.

Annual. Prefers rich, well-draining soil. Direct-sow from seed two weeks after the last spring frost and when day- and nighttime temperatures are 50°F (10°C) or greater. In cold climates, start inside two to four weeks before the last spring frost, using paper pots or other biodegradable containers so roots are disturbed as little as possible when transplanted. Cover seeds with 1/2 to 1 inch of soil, depending on seed size (see page 218) and sow one seed per container, planting out when soil temperatures are warm.

Summer squash are frost sensitive, requiring warm weather, plenty of sun and rich, fertile soil. I like to amend soil with a 2-inch blanket of aged manure and compost, then water deeply, either once every other day or once every three days depending on daytime highs. (Watering deeply encourages root development, making for a stronger root system and healthier, more resilient plants.) As with cucumbers, it's wise to plant seeds in mounds to ensure drainage.

I've also found that although I can pack together many other edibles, squash grow best with plenty of room. When sowing seeds in the garden, plant three seeds per planting area just in case some don't germinate, and then thin seedlings to one per every three feet or so. Floating row covers help protect plants from squash bugs and squash vine borers. Just be sure to remove the covers when plants start to bloom so pollinators can do their work.

> **Emily's Note**
>
> Male flowers tend to grow out toward the end of vines and appear to be attached directly to the stem. Female flowers grow closer to the center of plants and have an immature fruit that's visible at the base of the flower (waiting to be pollinated).

Pick

Harvest fruit when young and small for the best flavor and texture. For pattypan squash, this can be when fruits are 2 inches across, and 6 inches or more in length for zucchini. (That said, larger squash are better for stuffing and the quality of fruit varies depending on variety, so it's best to experiment.)

Cut or twist squash where the fruit meets the vine. Take them with or without flowers still attached. Squash plants produce both male and female flowers, both of which are edible; however, many say it's best to eat the male flowers because fruits develop from female flowers, and squash also produce more male than female flowers. Harvest as you would the fruit, by simply snapping or cutting them from the vine at the base of the flower. Gather them at the last possible minute and eat them within the day.

Fix

Although summer squash are milder in flavor than their winter relatives, they pair perfectly with the more vibrant flavors of tomatoes, basil and other fresh herbs. Make a pasta-free lasagna, replacing noodles with sliced squash. Add it to summer soups or grill it with lemon and garlic. Make zucchini fries, frittatas or an orzo salad with squash and feta.

Bake, steam or fry flowers. Make a squash flower soup with zucchini and corn, or stuff them with fresh herbs and cheese, bread them and fry lightly. They're also delicious sistered with cumin and coriander in quesadillas.

Before cooking with squash flowers, gently shake them free of bugs and any loose soil. Remove the pistil or stamen (the parts at the center of the flower) by simply pinching them free with your fingers. I generally wash them as little as possible or not at all if I've grown them myself. Unless they're cooked right away, they quickly disintegrate after being picked, as well as when they're exposed to moisture.

Varieties to Try

'**8 Ball**' and '**Ronde de Nice.**' Their shape makes them excellent for stuffing, but they can also be sliced for visual appeal. (You may also find them labeled "round zucchini.")

'**Cousa.**' These tend to be shorter and stouter than a zucchini and are slightly sweet with a light texture.

Pattypan or **scallop squash.** These disk-shaped squash with scalloped edges are some of the most flavorful. Try slicing them vertically or horizontally and cooking them slowly on the grill.

'**Sugar Loaf.**' An improved version of 'Delicata' squash, it's stockier in shape, sweeter and excellent for stuffing.

'**Zephyr.**' This variety is a cool cross between 'Delicata', yellow acorn, and yellow crookneck squash.

Zucchini. Also called courgettes, they come in shades of green and yellow, though they all have a similar taste. I especially love 'Costata Romanesco' for its ribbed stripes.

Summer Squash with Fresh Herbs & Capers

Bread it, fry it, stuff it, toss it in soups, pickle it, bake it or grill it. Or you can simply sauté it — definitely a favorite in my house. A quick sauté of summer squash with olive oil, then dressed with capers, toasted nuts and fresh herbs, marries with nearly anything you put next to it.

What You Need

1 splash or 2 extra-virgin olive oil
2 garlic cloves, minced
1 lb. summer squash, sliced into rounds about
    1/4 inch thick
Salt and pepper to taste
Chili flakes *optional
3 tbsp. toasted nuts, such as slivered almonds,
    pine nuts, pecans or hazelnuts
Small handful tender herbs such as basil, mint,
    chives or cilantro
2 tbsp. capers
Balsamic vinegar for drizzling

What You Do

1. Heat a splash of olive oil in a skillet. Once the oil is warm, add garlic and squash. Sauté over medium heat, letting the squash sear lightly on each side before flipping. It will take about 10 to 15 minutes for them to turn a warm shade of gold and become slightly crispy. I add a few cracks of salt and pepper and even some chili flakes during this process.
2. Toast nuts, and if you're working with larger-leafed herbs, chop them while squash cooks.
3. Once squash looks just right, remove from heat. Dress with nuts, herbs, capers and a drizzling of vinegar before serving. Serve warm or cool.

Serves 4.

PODS & BEANS

POLE, BUSH & RUNNER BEANS, SNAP & SNOW PEAS, FAVA OR BROAD BEANS

Legumes are the givers of the garden. They'll keep producing flowers and fruit as long as you keep picking them, and they can be grown strategically to maximize space. Some grow without end, sending vining tendrils in search of new territory all summer long (not unlike Jack and his beanstalk, so be careful your trellis isn't taller than your reach). Plant pole beans in the smallest gardens (where the only direction is up), train runner beans along archways, and grow snap peas when the weather is cool. There is a variety for every climate, need or recipe.

You'll soon find munching on a pea, bean pod or leafy shoot while picking sets one day apart from the next. There is something deeply wonderful and downright elemental about picking and eating from nature — and grazing in your garden in particular.

What You Should Know Before Planting

- Legumes are easy to grow, so no need to spend time or money on nursery starts.
- Some, like scarlet runner beans, are short-lived perennials, but most are annuals, many of which, like snap peas, are more frost hardy than others.

☙ If you have a slug or snail problem, consider sowing seeds in biodegradable containers, like paper pots, and plant them out once they're big enough to survive in the wider world of the garden.

☙ It only takes a few plants to yield what can sometimes feel like an unending, fabulous crop. Encourage flowering and fruiting with continual harvesting. This will also keep the bees, butterflies and hummingbirds coming.

☙ Shoots, flowers, young leaves, seeds and pods are all edible, while dried and more mature seeds require cooking.

☙ Overly mature green bean pods tend to get stringy and tough. I find it's best to let these dry on the vine, then shell and cook accordingly, or save them for planting next season's garden.

☙ Give vining legumes protection from wind with a sturdy climbing structure that's firmly anchored, and place them out of the direct path of prevailing winds.

☙ The entire lot can be rotated through your garden to fix nitrogen in soil naturally — no fertilizer required. The root systems, leaves and stems of legumes are nutrient rich and can be used as green manure. Leave roots of past crops in the soil to decompose, and add spent crops to compost to keep all the nutrients in your garden.

Pole, Bush & Runner Beans

Phaseolus vulgaris   Phaseolus coccineus

Sunny. This is the word my daughter uses to describe the flavor of green beans picked fresh off the vine and eaten on the spot. To find them hiding under leaves and rubbing shoulders with flowers is the first taste of joy; the second is in the two or three bites it takes to devour each bean, knowing she helped grow them from seed and tend to them as they wound their way up toward the sky — shining and radiant like the sunniest of days.

Plant

SUN. MODERATE TO REGULAR WATER.

Annual. Prefers rich, well-draining soil, although I don't fertilize before planting, but instead plant them where the crop before had a top dressing of compost or manure. Pole beans are not frost tolerant. However, scarlet runner beans are cold hardy and perennial in zones 6 and warmer with proper mulching. Direct-sow seeds, planting them straight in the garden, once all chance of frost is gone and nighttime temperatures stay above 55°F (13°C). Sow seeds about 1 inch deep, and consider sowing another round in midsummer for a late-summer harvest. Many varieties, such as French 'Rocquencourt' and dwarf 'Purple Teepee' beans, grow well in containers.

Give pole and runner beans a trellis, a teepee or even a fence with crop netting for tendrils to hold onto. Plan to grow about three vines per pole or per climbing area by sowing four to six seeds and thinning to three once they're established.

Bush beans, on the other hand, don't need staking or trellising. They grow well in containers, in raised beds or as part of an edible landscape. Sow seeds about 4 inches apart in rows or triangles, and ultimately space plants about 18 inches apart. If you have room and time, sow seeds successively about every three weeks.

Presoaking seeds before planting to speed up germination can actually make bean plants weaker. It's also important not to plant beans too early as they can rot in the ground — stick to direct-sowing seeds when the weather warms.

Pick

Check plants every few days for beans, lifting leaves and looking under trailing vines for fruit you may otherwise miss. Green beans are best when picked young as they become stringy and tough with age (a sign you need to harvest more frequently). If seeds are noticeably formed inside pods, leave them to dry on the vine so you can shell them for cooking or planting. Gather the pods with two hands to avoid damaging plants.

Fix

Eat green beans straight from the vine when young and tender. Add them to green or grain salads, or try them steamed, braised or baked. I love them roasted over a fire after tossing them with olive oil, garlic, salt and pepper. (They'll cook just right if double-wrapped in foil.) Or give them a lift by adding mushrooms, thyme, mint, peppery greens and cheese. They're delicious fermented or pickled, and they sister

well with miso, tempura and seeds. I honestly think it's impossible to go wrong. (They're just as easy to eat as they are to grow.)

When cooking purple beans, add a pinch of sugar to the cooking water to help keep their color. Young shoot tips and flowers are sweet and lovely when added to salads or used as a garnish.

Varieties to Try

'Borlotti.' This colorful bean is best eaten when dried.

'Gold Rush.' It makes sense to grow wax beans yourself. They're scarce at the market and exquisite when paired with green or purple snap beans.

'Kentucky Wonder.' This heirloom grown for its high-yielding crop is excellent fresh or dried.

'Nickel Filet.' These are small, delicate beans born on compact plants and considered a specialty of the green bean world.

'Royalty Purple Pod.' The purple pods of these snap beans are not only delicious but also striking against their green foliage. They're disease resistant and tolerant of cool weather.

'Scarlet Runner.' This variety bears gorgeous red flowers beloved by hummingbirds. Tasty as a small snap bean or when grown to maturity and dried. Perennial down to hardiness zone 7.

Left: Scarlet runner beans. Right: Borlotti beans.

Snap Peas & Snow Peas

Pisum sativum var. *macrocarpon*   *Pisum sativum* var. *saccharatum*

At the beginning of summer when the weather warms, it's time to replace snap peas with their more heat-tolerant cousins. I always make a note to plant more the next cool season — and each season, when I plant more, it's still not enough. The note is always the same, from one season to the next. They're a little bit of joy disguised as fruits.

Plant

SUN TO PART SHADE. MODERATE TO REGULAR WATER.

Annual. Prefers rich, well-draining soil. Direct-sow seeds six weeks before your last spring frost or when soils warm to 40°F (4°C) or warmer. They don't grow well when temperatures rise to about 80°F (27°C) in summer but can be planted again in fall in warmer climates (USDA hardiness zones 8 and warmer).

I often start peas in paper pots before transplanting out to the garden. Like other legumes, they're a favorite of slugs, snails and foraging birds. Starting them in biodegradable containers gives them a head start with the hope that they'll be able to fend for themselves once planted out. Where birds are particularly aggressive, consider wrapping chicken wire around the base of planting areas.

Give your peas a climbing trellis or cage for support, overplant so you're sure to have enough, and plan to pick and eat your way until production slows or the weather turns. I find that wrapping extra twine in among the legs of poles or cages gives delicate vines the extra support they need when first growing.

Snap peas in paper pots

It's also possible to grow snap and sugar peas as microgreens. Sow a carpet of seeds in a flat or tray, and once they're 2 or 3 inches tall, shear the shoots with scissors.

Pick

Harvest with two hands to prevent vines from breaking, using one to hold the vine while the other removes pods. Gather flowers and shoots as needed by snapping them free. (I generally grow plants for peas and sow a separate tray for greens and shoots — this way I don't miss a single pea.)

Fix

The fresher the better. If adding snow peas to a pasta, stir-fry, soup or sauté, toss them in at the last minute. If you don't plan to use them right away, soak pods in a bowl of water for 10 minutes to an hour before use to hydrate (like you would lettuce greens). Eat them fresh, pod and all, whenever possible. Chop them into salads, add them to grain dishes, and try them with mint and Meyer lemon, or with garlic and toasted sesame oil. They're delicious pickled too.

Varieties to Try

'**Cascadia.**' This variety of snap pea bears pods 3 inches in length that are wonderfully sweet and crisp. The plant grows to about 30 inches in height so doesn't require staking.

'**Dwarf Grey Sugar.**' Despite its name, this snow pea grows 4 to 5 feet tall. It bears lovely purple flowers and succulent, sweet pods.

'**Oregon Sugar Pod.**' This is one of the more productive varieties of snow peas along with Oregon Sugar Pod II, and it's disease resistant.

'**Super Sugar.**' Delicious raw, stir-fried or tossed in salads, this snap pea is reliably sweet and abundant.

Fava or Broad Beans

Vicia faba

It took a family visit to Italy for me to discover fava beans. I wondered how I could have missed them all these years, and even then, it took me several more years to learn to cook them with any skill. They're more work to cook than other beans because of the waxy coating surrounding each of the seeds, but it's worth the effort. They're unique, meaty and delicious in an earthy sort of way, bringing shape and flavor to meals that spring food to life.

Plant

SUN. MODERATE TO REGULAR WATER.

Annual. Not particular about soil quality, but well-draining soil of reasonable quality produces the best-tasting beans. Direct-sow six to eight weeks before your last spring frost in cold climates; in warm climates, plant in fall for an early spring crop. Space plants 6 to 12 inches apart, depending on variety. Tolerates light frosts.

Favas are a cool-weather crop that double as a great way to improve soil quality. These plants are so sturdy and keen to grow that they can be planted in dense soil to increase tilth and fix nitrogen. Plant them where little else will grow, and let them do the work of preparing the soil for future crops to come. Aphids will eventually find their way to any fava bean patch. Grow summer savory nearby to lure away the pests and ensure a plentiful harvest.

Pick

The flowers, shoots, young leaves and beans are all edible. Pick flowers and greens as needed, and harvest beans at various stages of growth, depending on the flavor you're after. Young beans that are about 2 inches long can be eaten whole. Let beans grow to about 4 to 5 inches long for shelling. The individual beans will be tender and bright green. Leave older beans for drying.

Fava bean in bloom

When growing fava beans strictly as a cover crop, it's best to cut them to the ground when they begin to flower and before they set fruit. Once plants set fruit, attention and nutrients are sent to support this process, leaving less in the roots to feed the soil. Add the tops to the compost pile, and leave the roots to decompose in the soil.

Fix

To shell fava beans for eating fresh or cooking, first remove the individual beans from their pods, then blanche the seeds in boiling water for 30 seconds. Immediately place them in cold water to stop the cooking process, and remove the waxy coating.

Fava bean hummus is always a treat, as is risotto with fava beans. Add them to soups or to pesto with mint, sauté them with dill, garlic and olive oil, or sprinkle over a pasta or spring salad. They pair well with fresh herbs of any kind, as well as greens or citrus.

Varieties to Try

'**Extra Precoce A Grano Violetto.**' An early fruiting variety from Italy, it yields long pods with beans that are sweet and a vibrant shade of purple.

'**Robin Hood.**' One of the more compact broad beans, this variety is ideal for containers or small space gardens.

'**Sweet Lorane.**' Their smaller seeds taste more like chickpeas.

'**Windsor.**' One of the most common varieties available in the United States. It's tall, growing to 2 to 4 feet (may require staking), and produces beans that are delicious and high in protein.

Fava Beans, Greens & Fresh Herb Tartine

Once I discovered fava beans, I began to experiment, first with a fava bean risotto, which is lovely yet time consuming. In search of a simpler way to enjoy their rich, nutty flavor, I began mixing them into spreads that were almost a cross between pesto and hummus — foods that I love having on hand in the fridge because they're fresh and delicious with everything.

Try this same spread on crackers, pasta, polenta, fish and roasted vegetables.

What You Need

2 cups shelled fresh fava beans
3 cups spring greens, such as arugula, mizuna, tatsoi or a combination, soaked and cleaned
Handful fresh herbs, such as basil, cilantro, parsley or mint (or a combination), coarsely chopped
1/2 cup extra-virgin olive oil, plus olive oil for drizzling
1 lemon cut into wedges
1/3 cup grated Parmigiano-Reggiano
2 small garlic cloves *optional
Salt and pepper to taste
1 baguette
Crumbled goat cheese

What You Do

1. Preheat oven to 350°F.
2. Blanche shelled fava beans in boiling water for 3 to 4 minutes. Immediately strain beans and pour into an ice bath to stop the cooking process. Once cool enough to handle, peel skins and place beans on a towel to dry.
3. Combine 3/4 of the beans, 2 1/2 cups greens, 1/2 or 3/4 of your fresh herbs, 1/2 cup oil, juice of 1/2 lemon, cheese, and 1 small garlic clove (*optional) in a food processor; chop so your final mixture isn't a puree. Add salt and pepper to taste.
4. Coarsely chop remaining fava beans and greens by hand and set aside.
5. Slice baguette, cut remaining garlic clove and rub on bread slices, and place on a baking sheet, toasting for about 8 minutes.
6. Top toasts with fava-bean and fresh-herb spread. Garnish with fresh herbs, chopped greens, extra fava beans, crumbled goat cheese, a squeeze of lemon, and a drizzle of olive oil.

Makes 2 cups.

EDIBLE PERENNIALS

ASPARAGUS, CHIVES,
RADICCHIO, RHUBARB

As you approach the town of Sonoma, California, from the north, there's a vineyard with a fabulous yet inconspicuous set of plantings skirting a low rock wall. You can't miss the row of fruit trees, but just beyond them is an equally long bed of asparagus. It's a frequent route for me, yet it was only recently that I recognized this clever use of space. Why not grow edibles like asparagus with landscape plantings? They're often just as interesting, if not more so, and their perennial nature makes them easy to care for. Plus, you get food!

This was my nonno's approach (my maternal great-grandfather, who immigrated to the United States from Italy). He practiced permaculture before it was called permaculture, optimizing what he could grow on his 200-acre homestead by working with nature. He grew tender plants close to home, planted orchards in open meadows with naturally occurring seeps, and tucked chestnut trees in where the soil and sun exposure were just right. But you don't need 200 acres; even something much smaller is big enough, and if it's well positioned, nature will do the work for you. There is an incredible number of edible perennials out there, so think of this chapter as a taste of what's possible.

Asparagus
Asparagus officinalis

A member of the lily family, the young shoots of homegrown asparagus are champions of spring. It can take two or three years to get them started, but once established, they'll produce edible spears for 20 years or more.

What You Should Know Before Planting

- Grows best in climates with winter freezes or periods of dryness.

- Asparagus needs space. It doesn't grow well in containers, but a raised bed 18 inches deep is good. Raised beds make weeding easier, and you can control soil quality from the outset. Another option is to place a wood frame around the asparagus planting area. Submerge the lower portion of the wood so it's anchored in place, and use it to define space while blending in with the landscape.

- Asparagus is monoecious, meaning there are female and male plants. Only the female plants produce seeds, but that's okay because we eat young shoots (not fruits). Consider growing only male plants. They produce more spears because they don't expend the energy required to grow fruit.

- Modern hybrids are more disease resistant. Growing heirlooms is romantic, but to make the most of your efforts, hybrids like 'Jersey Giant' and 'UC 157' are more care free.

- Enjoy six weeks of harvesting from mature plants — 25 plants produce plenty of fresh asparagus for a family of four, but 10 crowns could be a happy medium when weighing space, effort and return.

Plant

FULL SUN. REGULAR TO MODERATE WATER.

Perennial. Prefers rich, well-draining soil. Grow from crowns for more immediate results. Plant in spring as soon as soil can be worked. Prepare your planting area by removing all weeds. Loosen soil to a depth of 6 to 12 inches, then add 2 inches compost and work into soil. Space crowns 15 to 18 inches apart in rows that are 24 to 30 inches apart. Water regularly and deeply for the first two years. Grow in USDA hardiness zones 3 to 10.

It's possible to grow asparagus from seed. While far more cost effective, it's tricky and delays harvesting. Instead, look for crowns (pieces of asparagus roots) sold during a short spring window. They can be purchased up to three years old; however, older crowns are more expensive and more likely to suffer from shock after transplanting, so crowns are best purchased when they're a year old.

It's easiest to plant in rows, digging a trench 12 inches deep and 12 inches wide. (Individual trenches will just touch.) Before digging, loosen the first 6 to 12 inches of soil and work in an inch or two of organic compost. Sprinkle in some balanced vegetable fertilizer. Greensand and rock phosphate are also good additions, ensuring adequate potassium and phosphorus for the growing roots.

Form little mounds of soil about 6 inches tall and 18 inches apart inside each trench. Place asparagus crowns on top of these mounds, draping the roots over the edges. Cover the crowns with 2 inches of soil, and water well.

As asparagus grows, continue to cover the growth with soil, and water well until the soil level of each row is above the surrounding soil level. Eventually the soil over the crowns will settle and match the rest of the planting area.

Maintain a weed-free planting area, and cut back asparagus fronds to soil level only once they've turned yellow in fall. Remove leaf trimmings from the garden to reduce risk of spreading disease. Top-dress with a mix of compost and manure in the fall; in colder climates, cover with an insulating layer of seedless straw or leaf mold.

Pick

Harvesting too much too soon will weaken plants. Wait until the second year of growth to harvest asparagus, and then harvest only spears that are wider in diameter than a pencil, for just one week. Harvest for two to four weeks in the third year, and for six to eight continuous weeks in the fourth year and beyond.

Gather asparagus spears when they're 5 to 7 inches tall, cutting at soil level with a sharp knife or snapping them free with your fingers. Plan to harvest every other day or more when conditions are right, but don't be greedy. Once your harvest period is past, leave any remaining shoots. This growth is a critical stage of the asparagus life cycle as this is when plants have an opportunity to capture and store energy from the sun.

Opposite: Spring harvest of asparagus, kale and carrots.

Fix

Asparagus is incredibly versatile. Grill, simmer, steam, blanche, roast, batter or stir-fry it for delicious, easy treatment from garden to table. You can even slice it very thin and add to a fresh salad. I personally love it paired with lemon and feta after steaming, or with olive oil and Parmesan when roasting. It's also fabulous battered and rolled into sushi.

Chives

Allium schoenoprasum

It's always a wonder to me to see a garden without chives, partly because they basically grow themselves. They not only are incredibly hardy and delicious but also bear beautiful lavender flowers that are good to eat. Like other bulbs, they're some of the first to take hold in early spring, with their grassy leaves breathing new life into the garden.

Plant

SUN. MODERATE WATER.

Perennial. Prefers rich, well-draining soil, but not incredibly fussy if planted in soil of moderate quality. Sow from seed or plant from bulbs, starts or divisions for most immediate use. Direct-sow seeds four to six weeks before your last spring frost. Plant bulbs, starts or divisions about 8 inches apart. Divide once every three years and keep well weeded. Grows well in USDA hardiness zones 3 to 10.

Plant chives in a container or raised bed for the easiest care, keeping them weed free, especially free of grasses. (It's nearly impossible to separate grasses from chives once they take hold.) Grow them as a neat border in the landscape or garden bed.

Fertilize in spring with a balanced fertilizer or compost tea, go light on the mulch to improve air circulation near the soil level, and water deeply but infrequently to encourage the growth of strong, healthy roots. For a garlicky twist, grow garlic chives, *Allium tuberosum.*

Pick

Harvest leaves from the outside in as needed. Use scissors to cut clumps of leaves 2 inches above soil level. Pinch or cut flowers for salads and garnishes. Cut back the entire plant once all the flowers fade.

Fix

Freeze excess leaves (chive leaves lose their flavor when dried), and dry flowers to add to vinegars and dressings. Use fresh chives in sauces, potato and yogurt dishes, omelets, soups and breads. Add them to cheeses, fresh summer salads and fish. Put them on anything you'd season with onion (in my house, that's nearly everything) as they offer the fresh flavor of onion without the bite.

Radicchio

Cichorium intybus

Radicchio demands a bold and adventuresome palate, one that's unafraid to leave a sweet tooth behind. Also known as Italian chicory, radicchio is a close cousin of endives and other chicories, which include frisée and escarole. All share the same family as lettuce but are instead far more robust and bitter.

This can be a welcome contrast to the sweeter flavors of summer just left behind, marking the seasons while balancing the menu — and at just the right time.

Plant

SUN TO PART SHADE. REGULAR WATER.

Perennial, though can be grown as an annual (particularly in cold climates). Prefers rich, well-draining soil. Direct-sow six to eight weeks before your first fall frost, or start indoors and transplant out once true leaves develop. In cool summer climates, or when growing in shade, start indoors four to six weeks before the last average spring frost, and transplant out when true leaves develop. Germination is best when temperatures range from 60 to 75°F (16 to 24°C). Grows well in containers, on raised beds or as landscape plantings. Thrives in USDA hardiness zones 4 and warmer.

In most climates, radicchio is a cool-season crop planted in summer and harvested in fall and winter — it can even be harvested throughout winter from under a blanket of snow. It will bolt and become bitter with summer heat if planted too early, unless it gets some shade. Once established, grow radicchio as a perennial by cutting heads just above soil level with a sharp knife. Protect the roots and surrounding soil with a thick layer of mulch, straw or leaves, and plants will grow a fresh round of greens come spring.

> ## Emily's Note
> Modern hybrids of radicchio are less fussy to grow and quicker to mature than traditionally grown heirlooms, but all are tasty.

Pick

Harvest individual leaves as needed, or encourage plants to form heads with less aggressive harvesting. If plants are having trouble forming heads, cut leaves to the ground. New growth is more likely to form a dense head of greens, perfect for roasting or grilling.

Fix

Add young or finely chopped leaves to fresh salads and complement with sweeter varieties of greens. Try it pickled, fermented or cooked. (Cooking reduces bitterness.) Steam; sauté with garlic, chili peppers and olive oil; grill or roast; or pair with a grain salad. It's delicious seared in a skillet and drizzled with a balsamic vinegar reduction and added to pasta or risotto or sistered with white beans.

Varieties to Try

'Chioggia Red Preco No. 1.' Quick to mature, this variety is adapted to spring and summer planting and is slow to bolt.

'Indigo Hybrid.' This variety grows into bright burgundy heads and performs well in all seasons.

'Palla Rossa Mavrik.' It likes cool weather and short days, and it overwinters well.

Rhubarb

Rheum rhabarbarum

One of the first heralds of spring, the colossal leaves of rhubarb unfurl from the ground as if from nowhere. It's one of those amazing herbaceous perennials, stretching open new leaves after hibernating through the darkest days of winter. In fall, the foliage with tender, red stalks dies back, sending any remaining energy down to its root system to lie in wait for spring. An entirely new set of leaves is born when conditions are just right. After only a few short weeks, harvesting can begin.

Plant

SUN. MODERATE TO REGULAR WATER.

Perennial. Prefers rich, well-draining soil that's high in organic matter. While it can be grown from seed, it's best to plant rhubarb from dormant root divisions in spring. Plant a division or crown 1 to 3 inches deep as soon as soil can be worked. Cover with soil, and mulch and water well. Space 2 to 3 inches apart. USDA hardiness zones 3 to 8. (I've grown it successfully in zone 10, although its flavor is not as intense.)

The trick with rhubarb is to give it a spot where it can thrive for a good, long while. Like asparagus, rhubarb is a long-lived perennial, so it's best to choose a planting site carefully. If you're working with clay soil, loosen and amend soil well before planting to improve drainage, or plant in a garden bed. However, rhubarb is a space hog, covering about 4 square feet of soil, so you may not want to give up precious garden space for a single plant — it's best to think of it as a plant for an edible landscape.

Rhubarb is easy to care for. It grows best when it receives long periods of cold (40°F/ 4°C or below) in winter. It doesn't need regular fertilizing, although I like to top-dress it with a 2-inch layer of aged manure once a year, ringing the root crown without covering it. It will also appreciate being divided after five to 10 years.

You'll know it's time to divide rhubarb when it begins to lose its luster and stems look thin and crowded. To do it, simply lift the root system while it's still dormant in early spring and before new leaves begin to develop. First, loosen surrounding soil by digging around the roots, and pull the entire plant from the ground. Then, separate the root crown into pieces, making sure there are one to three leaf buds per division. While it sounds harsh, you may need to whack at it with a shovel or small hatchet as the root ball can become woody with age. Replant one or more of the divisions, and share the rest with friends!

Pick

Gather rhubarb stalks by giving a gentle pull and slight twist while holding near the base of the stem, and the stem will come free from the root crown. Harvest in spring, taking from plants that are two years or older. Like asparagus, rhubarb needs all its energy to develop a healthy root system when getting started. Harvest for just one or two weeks in the second year and for eight to 10 weeks in subsequent years. Plan to wrap up your harvest season by about June, though it can technically continue to be harvested until the first freeze. Take only one-third of the total stalks.

Rhubarb leaves are not only inedible, they're toxic, containing high concentrations of oxalic acid. Before you prepare stems, cut leaves away from the stalks and compost the trimmings. Harvest stalks as needed for the best flavor and freshness, and prune flowers as they emerge to encourage leaf growth.

Fix

Both mouthwatering and lip puckering, the tart yet sweet flavors of rhubarb waken the taste buds. It's a welcome change from the winter menu, geared toward pies, tarts and jams. If slivered thinly, it pairs well with other veggies, like radishes, and a sweet vinaigrette for a fresh twist on salad. A simple rhubarb syrup is delicious with seltzer or stronger beverages such as rum. Rhubarb pairs well with maple syrup, honey, strawberries, raspberries, apples, cinnamon, citrus, creamy dishes and yogurt.

More Edible Perennials

Artichoke, *Cynara scolymus*. A thistle hardy to USDA zone 6 and warmer. Grow them in a border, raised bed or container.

French sorrel, or **common sorrel**, *Rumex acetosa*. This tangy, leafy green is hardy in zones 4 to 9.

Fruit trees: Fig, pomegranate, apple, pineapple guava, peach, lemon and other citrus grow well in containers 10 to 15 gallons in size. Look for dwarf varieties, trees grown on cordon rootstock or grafted trees with more than one variety per tree.

Ground cherry, *Physalis spp.* Plants bear tomato-like fruits but are not frost hardy, though they happily reseed in the coldest of climates. Perennial in frost-free climates, otherwise a self-seeding annual.

Jerusalem artichoke, or **sunchoke**, *Helianthus tuberosus*. Its nutty, potato-like tubers and gorgeous flowers are hardy in zones 3 to 9.

Lovage, *Levisticum officinale*. Bears a strong celery flavor but can grow up to 6 feet tall! Hardy to USDA zone 4 and warmer, it's a fabulous edible perennial.

Purple tree collard, or **tree kale**, *Brassica oleracea* var. *Acephala*. It's long living, provides a continuous supply of greens and is easily grown from cuttings. Hardy to zone 7 and warmer.

Saffron, or **autumn crocus**, *Crocus sativus*. One of the first flowering bulbs to emerge in spring, you can collect the pollen for your favorite risotto.

Scarlet runner beans, *Phaseolus coccineus*. These fuzzy green beans are best eaten when tender and young. Plants bear bright red flowers that are a favorite of hummingbirds. Hardy in zones 7 to 11, or grow as an annual in colder climates.

Watercress, *Nasturtium officinale*. This aquatic or semi-aquatic perennial is grown for its nutritious leafy greens. Give it sun to part shade, plant in containers or a water feature, and grow indoors or out. Grow in USDA hardiness zones 3 to 11.

Spiced Rhubarb Compote

There are two defining qualities to this recipe: First, it's a cinch to make. There's really no way you can mess it up, no matter what proportions you use — unless you burn it to a crisp (something I've been known to do, and in which case, you'll need to start over). Second, it's the perfect mix of savory, sweet and sour, and it's fabulous with anything creamy or crumbly.

What You Need

1 1/2 to 2 lb. rhubarb, washed and chopped into 2-inch pieces

1/4 cup maple syrup or honey (I find honey holds together a little better, but I love the flavor of maple syrup and sometimes sweeten with a mix of the two.)

2 oranges, 1 sliced in rounds and 1 juiced

2 star anise pods

3 or 4 whole green cardamom pods

1 vanilla bean cut lengthwise, seeds separated (though seeds may not be evident) *optional

2 cinnamon sticks

3/4-inch piece ginger, thickly shaved *optional

What You Do

1. Preheat oven to 400°F.
2. Mix ingredients in a large bowl or baking dish.
3. Bake until rhubarb is tender, about 10 to 12 minutes.
4. Serve warm or cool over ice cream or yogurt.

Note: If you're not a fan of the stringy texture of rhubarb, I suggest chopping it into smaller chunks before combining it with the other ingredients.

Serves 6 to 8.

BERRIES

BLUEBERRIES, CANE BERRIES, STRAWBERRIES

When I was young, my mother's prize garden was a patch of strawberries. It was my job to run out after school to see what had ripened since the day before. I'd move out of the way of my shadow to let in the glow of fading light in order to find what I was looking for, lifting leaves to reveal the red, juicy goodness that the birds had somehow missed.

It wasn't long before my parents added raspberries to the mix. My father built a set of four raised beds, and in a year or two they were brimming with berries. Next came two more beds for blueberries. Berries are like that. The adage *less is more* doesn't apply; instead it's just the opposite. More is more — of everything! The dividends are paid out as sublime moments in the garden spent tending, picking and eating.

Blueberries

Vaccinium spp.

The key to success when growing blueberries is choosing the right varieties for your region and climate. (This is where you can lean on your neighbors or local nursery for advice.)

Plant

SUN TO PART SHADE. MODERATE TO REGULAR WATER.

Perennial. Prefers moderate-quality, acidic soil with excellent drainage. Grows best with a soil pH between 4 and 5.5. Acidify soil for in-ground plantings by amending with elemental sulfur, a naturally occurring mineral, or by planting in containers or raised beds and beginning with an organic acidic planting mix. Work soil well and bury plants to just below their original potting depth. Plant spacing depends on variety. Grow from USDA hardiness zones 2 to 10, depending on species.

For in-ground gardens, test soil pH before planting (send soil samples to a testing center and request organic soil amendment recommendations). Grow more than one variety — as cross-pollination produces more, and better-tasting, fruit — and choose species and cultivars best suited to your climate and garden. Look for varieties with different fruiting periods to stretch out your harvest, and when planting in containers, look for compact or dwarf varieties.

Spread a 2- to 3-inch layer of mulch over the planting area to protect soil and reduce weed growth. Water well after planting, giving blueberries at least one deep watering per week. Fertilize in early spring using a balanced organic fertilizer designed for blueberries, or a seed meal like soybean or alfalfa, and prune plants when they're three years old or older. Prune when dormant in late winter, and clean up deadwood and cross-branching to keep plants open and airy. Prune lowbush blueberries to the ground once every three years or so.

Emily's Note

Berries are versatile and grow just as well in a landscape as they do in a kitchen garden. Consider blueberries as foundation plantings for a border that is both gorgeous and edible, or grow cane berries as an edible hedge. Both are fabulous companion plants, attracting pollinators and other wildlife.

Pick

You'll know fruit is ripe and ready to harvest when berries fall into your hand or come free easily. Ultra-ripe fruit is the best-tasting fruit. Berries will keep longer if they're stored dry and not washed.

Fix

The best way to eat blueberries is straight off the vine or made into pie, jam or syrup. I use as little sugar as possible with any recipe so I can taste the fruit (not the sugar). And I always test fruit before and during any process that requires the addition of sugar so I don't overdo it. (I never follow a recipe when it comes to fruit and sugar proportions, except with jams and jellies, because no two harvests are alike.)

You can also add blueberries to pancakes, muffins, smoothies, cakes, crumbles, creams, scones and tarts. Try them fresh or dried on salads, or use them to make fruit leather or a zesty shrub (drinking vinegar) for a fresh summer cocktail.

Opposite: An upcycled bicycle wheel makes a perfect structure for hanging protective bird netting.

Varieties to Try

Lowbush, *Vaccinium angustifolium* or *V. myrtilloides*. Compact bushes native to colder regions of North America, they make a fabulous edible hedge and can be grown in part shade. They generally produce smaller fruits that are best for baking. Try 'Burgundy,' 'Top Hat' or 'Brunswick.'

Northern highbush, *Vaccinium corymbosum*. Native to eastern North America, they can grow up to six feet tall, bear sweet, tangy fruits and have gorgeous fall foliage. Try 'Legacy,' 'Bluecrop,' 'Darrow' or 'Bluegold.'

Rabbiteye, *Vaccinium ashei*. Growing 20 feet tall or more if not pruned and native to southeastern United States, rabbiteyes are named for their fruits, which turn from pink to blue. They grow best in climates with mild winters. Plan to prune vigorously the first few years after planting. 'Climax,' 'Baldwin' and 'Premier' are just three of many delicious rabbiteye cultivars.

Southern highbush. These are cultivars designed to thrive in regions with mild winters and hot summers. 'Southmoon,' 'Jubilee' and 'Jewel' are just a few.

Cane Berries
Rubus spp.

This is a broad group of berries that grow from canes or stick-like stems, including raspberries, blackberries, marionberries, boysenberries and loganberries. Their growth habits vary from trailing to erect, and many benefit from trellising (which also makes the job of harvesting and caring for them easier). Most need room to move and spread; however, recent cultivars designed to be compact and grown in containers mean you don't need an expansive garden to enjoy fresh berries.

Plant

SUN. MODERATE WATER.

Perennial. Prefers moderate to rich soil with excellent drainage. Plant from cuttings, starts or bare root stock. Amend in spring with a top dressing of all-purpose, organic fertilizer, and ring with a fresh layer of mulch, giving the canes a wide berth. Space plantings 2 to 4 inches apart, depending on the variety. For in-ground and raised-bed plantings, water young plants deeply once a week and mature plants once every 10 days to two weeks. Let container plantings dry out between waterings, and plan to water at least twice a week, especially when temperatures rise.

Before you plant, prepare and amend your planting area with compost, aged manure or leaf mold, and if necessary, install a trellis system. Think of the trellis system as a method for supporting trailing vines, improving air circulation and increasing sun exposure. It can be as simple as two posts placed at either end of a planting row with line or wire strung between the posts, or an arbor for container plantings.

Give cane berries their own planting beds or containers to decrease maintenance. Bury plants at the same depth as they were originally planted or, if you're using bare root stock, to just above the root crown. Train and prune vines as needed any time of year, keeping them tidy. Although cane berries are perennial, the canes themselves are biennial, dying after the second year of growth. Most cane berries produce fruit on second-year canes.

Plan to prune all spent second-year canes, cutting at or just above ground level in fall or early spring. (You'll recognize which ones these are because they wither, turn brown and become pithy.) When patches become thick with canes, remove the smaller ones (even if they're in their first year), leaving three to six vigorous canes per foot.

Pick

Homegrown berries always taste better than store bought (because you picked them yourself).

You'll know fruit is ripe when berries come freely off the vine and have a melt-in-your-mouth sweetness. Pick daily or as often as possible when fruit is coming in. Dry fruit can store for a few days in the fridge. As with other berries, wait to wash until moments before eating or cooking with them. For longer storage, freeze fruit on a cookie sheet in single layers (to maintain their shape and integrity) before piling them into freezer containers.

Fix

First, eat them straight off the vine, then rustle up your favorite jam, cake or pie recipe. Try them on pizza, tossed in salads or blended into a smoothie or ice cream. Make a sauce for meats or a fruity dressing, or add them to a peach crumble. They also make the perfect garnish for anything else that's in season.

Types of Cane Berries

Blackberries. I always keep a rough map of where to pick wild berries and, because they're so precious, keep a plant or two at home. New cultivars of thornless blackberries have taken the mess out of growing them, making them prickle-free and easy to grow in containers. 'Apache,' 'Navaho' and 'Arapaho' are all excellent choices and can be trained to grow on a trellis, keeping them compact while increasing surface area and yields. 'Marion,' or marionberry, is another favorite, although it's not thornless. Plant in late fall to spring, or through the summer if gardening in containers. Hardy from USDA zones 5 to 10.

Boysenberries. A cross between four *Rubus* species, the best boysenberries are both super sweet and super tart and make fabulous pies. It's an early fruiting variety, cropping from May to July. This is one you'll be lucky to find at your farmer's market, so your best bet is to grow them yourself. Look for thornless varieties for easiest care, and plant in fall or spring. Grows best in hardiness zones 5 to 10.

Loganberries. Another raspberry and blackberry cross, loganberries bear a deep red to purple fruit compared with the dark purple of boysenberries. They're prized for their disease resistance, undemanding nature and sweet flavor and typically crop in August and September. Plant in fall or anytime if growing in containers. They perform best with trellising and when grown in hardiness zones 5 to 10.

Raspberries. Delicate and delicious, these tart yet sweet berries have a flavor all their own. There are summer-bearing and ever-bearing cultivars, but be prepared for any raspberry planted in-ground to spread vigorously via its root system. Some of my favorite cultivars include 'Fall Gold,' a sweet, golden fall fruiting berry; 'Caroline,' an ever-bearing variety fruiting in June and again in fall; and 'Killarney,' which is highly disease resistant, fruits early and is fabulous in preserves. 'Raspberry Shortcake' grows well in patio containers and fruits in midsummer. Plant bare root stock or starts in spring. Thrives in USDA hardiness zones 3 to 10, depending on the cultivar.

Strawberries

Fragaria spp.

The range and number of strawberry cultivars are limitless. There are June-bearing, ever-bearing and day-neutral cultivars (all a form of *Fragaria ∑ ananassa*). There are strawberries that set runners and strawberries that don't, such as with many alpine strawberries (*Fragaria vesca*).

   June-bearing cultivars set fruit in spring as soon as the weather warms, although, in mild climates, they continue to fruit far past June and generally produce more bountiful crops than ever-bearing or day-neutral cultivars. They also tend to set more runners than ever-bearing or day-neutral cultivars. Ever-bearing cultivars are tried-and-true continual producers and are well suited to containers and hanging baskets.

Plant

SUN TO PART SHADE (DEPENDING ON CULTIVAR). MODERATE TO REGULAR WATER.

Perennial. Prefers rich, well-draining soil. Plant starts or daughter plants clipped from runners for most immediate harvests. (It's possible to grow alpine strawberries from seed, but it takes patience.) Plant F. ananassa *cultivars in November and* F. vesca *cultivars*

in spring. Space about 8 inches apart, depending on cultivar. Grow in USDA hardiness zones 3 to 10, depending on cultivar.

Strawberries are incredibly hardy and grow whether you pay attention to them or not. I find the biggest problem is keeping runners under control, which is why it helps to give strawberries their own containers or planting areas and plenty of rooting depth, and to amend at least once a year with a balanced organic fertilizer or aged manure. Clip runners to ensure energy stays with the mother plant, and protect fruit from birds (see page 254). Plan to replace mother plants once every three to five years, or grow them as annuals and rotate with brassicas to naturally ward off common diseases.

Pick

Harvest strawberries when perfectly ripe and before birds find them. The cool hours of the morning are generally best for increasing shelf life, although grazing whenever you visit the garden is a must.

Fix

Tarts, cakes, jams, creams and pies are where strawberries shine. Chop and mix them into popsicles, smoothies, sorbet or crème brûlée. Add a sweet twist to dressings or toss into a savory salad. Pair with spring greens, mesclun mix, almonds and chèvre. For something a little different, add them to chutney, risotto or pizza.

Emily's Note

Most strawberry cultivars have beautiful fall foliage and make fabulous land-scape plants. If you don't have room in your kitchen garden, consider planting them along borders or as ground cover.

Varieties to Try

Alpine strawberry cultivars. 'White Delight, 'Mignonette,' 'Improved Rugen' and 'Yellow Wonder.' Though not heavy producers like the others, alpine straw-berries are scrumptious, don't set runners (making my job easier) and tolerate some shade. The white varieties have the added benefit of being overlooked by birds.

Ever-bearing cultivars. 'Quinault,' 'Tribute,' 'Pineberry' and 'Tristar.'

Day-neutral cultivars. 'Seascape,' 'Albion,' 'Aromas' and 'Evie.'

June-bearing cultivars. 'Jewel,' 'Sequoia,' 'EarliGlo' and 'Cabot.'

Summer Berry Shrub

My favorite recipes are the ones that don't require a recipe. Instead, the ingredients and ratios provide a road map to the end product. This is that recipe — a zesty, fruity vinegar beverage that may become your next obsession, and all you have to do is get the ratios right. The flavor combinations are up to you or, as is usually the case in the garden, whatever happens to be ripe for picking.

What You Need

1 part berries or other soft fruit

1 part sugar (Try white or raw sugar, or experiment with honey, maple syrup or agave)

1 part vinegar (Experiment with apple cider, balsamic, champagne, coconut or red wine vinegar or a combination. Balsamic pairs incredibly well with berries but can be cut with cider or red wine vinegars. Consider the flavor intensity of your fruit when selecting a vinegar.)

What You Do

1. Gently wash berries and place in a bowl with an equal amount of sugar. Mix together, lightly mashing fruit to blend.
2. Cover the mixture and refrigerate for at least 6 hours, but 48 hours is even better. You should see syrup collecting in the bottom of the bowl. I find it helpful to stir the fruit and sugar occasionally, otherwise the sugar has a tendency to collect at the bottom.
3. Stir and then strain the syrup from the mixture using a fine-mesh colander, and press on solids to express remaining syrup. If there's extra sugar in the bottom of the bowl, scrape it into the syrup.
4. Whisk in vinegar until evenly blended, then pour the shrub into a clean bottle or canning jar. Cap it, shake vigorously, date the bottle and refrigerate.
5. It's ready to drink right away, but the flavors soften and become less vinegar-forward if you let it sit in the fridge for a few days to a week. Stores in the fridge for at least two months.
6. Add fresh shrub to seltzer water or lemonade, freeze it into popsicles with edible flowers, or make it into a wonderfully refreshing cocktail. For a cocktail, try pairing it with your favorite liquor and combine with seltzer, fresh fruit and herbs.

Shrubs were historically fermented, but this recipe isn't — start over if your shrub bubbles or becomes slimy.

Serving size depends on proportions.

EDIBLE FLOWERS & COMPANION PLANTS

BORAGE, CALENDULA, NASTURTIUM, SCENTED GERANIUM, SUNFLOWER, VIOLA

There is more than one thing at work in a garden. Some might argue that the soil is the heart and soul of growing, but what would a garden be without flowers? Without fragrance and color, the sound of bees, ladybug sightings or the quiet work of butterflies? And how lucky we are that there's such a long list of edible flowers that pair well with herbs and vegetables. When you include these companion plants in your garden, they'll help you manage pests, create pollinator havens and support the overall health of your garden — all while looking pretty in the process.

Companion plants are combinations of plants that grow better together. They have a variety of roles, from repelling bad bugs and attracting good ones to masking the scent of one plant with another. The benefits can also be structural. For instance, vining plants like pole beans can find support in tall, sturdy plants like sunflowers; squash can be grown to trail along at their feet, protecting soil moisture and preventing weeds from growing.

Borage
Borago officinalis

Borage is a bee magnet. Its delicate, star-shaped flowers practically drip with nectar, providing a banquet for bees and hoverflies. Borage also attracts predatory insects that feed on pests such as tomato hornworms, and many gardeners believe it improves the flavor of crops such as strawberries because of its ability to add trace minerals to soil. Though flavor is subjective and dependent on a variety of factors, it's worth testing for yourself.

Plant

SUN. MODERATE WATER.

Annual. Not picky about soil, is fairly drought tolerant and is easy to grow from seed. Direct-sow seeds one to two weeks before your last spring frost and when soils are warm. In mild climates, scatter-sow seeds in fall for spring germination. Not recommended for indoor seeding and transplanting because of its taproot, though you could try starting borage in paper pots six weeks before your last spring frost. Bury seeds 1/4 to 1/2 inch deep. Space plants 12 inches apart for optimal growth.

Borage is a prolific self-seeder, and its leaves become pricklier as they mature, making it challenging to remove from the garden — it could easily overrun your veggie plot if you're not careful. Dedicate a planting bed, border or deep container to borage to help keep it under control. Learn to identify its young leaves so you can easily weed it (and eat it) when found growing in unwanted locations.

Pick
Harvest leaves when young and cook as you would chard or spinach. Gather and graze on flowers as needed.

Fix
Use young borage leaves as a substitute for chard, spinach or nettles. Infuse leaves in a tea, or chop finely and wilt before adding to soups, pasta dishes, quesadillas or calzones. Flowers have a wonderful cucumber flavor. Eat them fresh, tossed in salads, infused in water, as a garnish or candied and added to cookies and cakes.

Calendula

Calendula officinalis

My first experience with calendula was when I was studying herbal medicine. I carefully dried its petals and infused them into an oil that I later added to salves and lotions. It quickly evolved from one of my most loved healing plants to one of my most loved garden plants. Calendula attracts pollinators and beneficial insects, like ladybugs. It also repels aphids, whiteflies and other pests, like tomato hornworms.

Like many edible flowers, borage (opposite) and calendula (left) are attractive to both people and pollinators.

Plant

SUN. MODERATE TO REGULAR WATER.

Short-lived perennial grown as an annual. Prefers rich, well-draining soil but isn't terribly picky. Easy to plant from seed. In mild climates, cast seeds in the fall or direct-sow two to four weeks before the last spring frost. In cold climates, start indoors six to eight weeks before your last spring frost. Bury seeds 1/4 to 1/2 inch deep, and keep seeds evenly moist through the germination process.

Plant at the ends of raised beds, tucked into corners or along borders. Grow with tomatoes, basil, asparagus and beans to lure pests away from crops. Keep plants healthy by pruning browning stems and leaves.

Pick
Gather whole flowers or flower petals as needed.

Fix
Petals are lovely in salads, soups, stews and breads. Use fresh or dried petals as a saffron substitute. Dry flowers for use in healing, topical creams and oils, or add them to tea.

Nasturtium

Tropaeolum majus

Versatile and elegant, nasturtiums add spice to the garden. Leaves, flowers and seeds are all edible and peppery in flavor. Nasturtiums are also dynamic companion plants. Their trailing nature allows them to protect garden soil, keeping it cool and retaining moisture when temperatures rise. They attract beneficial insects, and pollinators such as bees, and provide habitat for important predatory insects like spiders and ground beetles. They also lure black aphids away from vegetables. Grow them with tomatoes, radishes, melons, brassicas and cucumbers.

Plant

SUN TO LIGHT SHADE. MODERATE WATER.

Annual. Not picky about soil. Direct-sow seeds two weeks after your last spring frost. In hot regions, like the South West, sow in fall for a winter bloom. Bury seeds 1/2 inch deep (seeds require darkness to sprout). Presoak seeds overnight to speed germination. Space plants 6 to 12 inches apart. Freely volunteers in mild climates, doing the work of planting itself from one season to the next.

Grow strategically to deter pests and lure aphids away from susceptible crops. Plant in corners, along edges or in containers for a beautiful effect.

Pick

Harvest leaves, flowers and seeds as needed. I find it's best to pick leaves and flowers as late in the cooking process as possible so they're at their freshest. Look for seeds beneath plants, leaving a few to volunteer, and gather the rest for cooking.

Fix

Seeds make wonderful capers when pickled. Toss fresh leaves and flowers in salads for a spicy taste, or chop and cook them lightly. Sister with parsley, cheese and tomatoes on a summer sandwich, or try them in quesadillas, in savory pastries or as a garnish.

nasturtium pods

Scented Geranium

Pelargonium spp.

The flowers of scented geraniums are dazzling, but their deeper appeal is their leaves with scents of nutmeg, pineapple, ginger, lemon, apricot, apple and rose. Cook with cinnamon, lime or chocolate mint varieties, and enjoy pungent varieties, like citronella, simply for their fragrance.

Plant

SUN. MODERATE WATER.

Perennial in USDA hardiness zones 9 and up. Prefers rich soil with excellent drainage. Add extra mulch or compost to improve drainage as needed. Grow from cuttings or starts. Water deeply once a week, depending on weather, letting soil dry out in between. Plant out in the garden or in containers in warm climates. In colder climates, grow in containers so it's easy to bring plants inside when temperatures dip below freezing.

Scented geraniums will draw Japanese beetles away from roses, fruit trees and even green beans. Plant strategically to best protect your plants.

Pick

Gather leaves by gently separating leaf stems from the main stem. Snap them off with your thumb and forefinger at a right angle to the main stem, or cut with clippers. Flowers are edible, too, and can be harvested as needed.

Fix

Let fragrance lead the way. Infuse scented geranium leaves in simple syrups, teas, flavored sugars, baked goods and roasted veggies or soups to release the aromatic oils. Like bay leaves, it's generally not advised to eat the leaves themselves, but use them to enhance flavors. For quick, on-the-fly enjoyment, gently bruise or crush the leaves before adding to a thirst-quenching lemonade or cocktail. To experience deeper, more complex flavors, make a simple syrup or tea. Flowers are also edible and can be crystallized and added to sorbets, ice creams and desserts.

Sunflower
Helianthus spp.

Sunflowers have a wonderful way of requiring little but giving so much in return. Their sturdy, vertical nature is perfect for the smallest of gardens, allowing them to double as a support for climbing pole beans. They're a bee favorite and, of course, produce lovely cut flowers as well as seeds for saving and eating.

Plant

SUN. MODERATE TO REGULAR WATER.

Annual. Prefers moderate to rich well-draining soil. Direct-sow seeds one to two weeks after your last spring frost, or start indoors two to four weeks before your last spring frost. If starting indoors, it's best to grow them in individual paper pots so their roots are disturbed as little as possible when transplanting. Plant seeds 1/4 to 1 inch deep depending on size of seed. Spacing depends on size of plant at maturity.

Sunflowers are easy to grow and happy to volunteer in mild climates. Look for their telltale leaves emerging in spring, and move them around your garden for optimal placement, planting them on the north side of beds so they don't shade out other sun-loving plants. Group them together for a shock of color, and hope the squirrels and birds don't get to the seeds before you do!

Pick

Harvest seeds once flower petals start to dry and fall away and seeds look plump and mature. If birds are a problem, or you're worried too many seeds will fall to the ground before harvesting, try covering flower heads with a paper bag or cheese-cloth, giving seeds more time to mature. When they are ready, cut the stem below the flower and bring it inside. Pry seeds to begin releasing them. Once a few have come free, they'll all quickly fall away. If you don't plan to eat all the seeds you've grown, leave extras in the garden for birds and other animals.

Fix

Save some seeds for planting next season, and eat the rest raw or roasted. You can also soak the seeds in salt water for added flavor. Combine 1/8 cup salt per quart of water and soak overnight. Once seeds are fully dry, roast them for about 30 minutes at 300°F. Store them in an airtight container in your pantry.

Viola

Viola odorata   Viola tricolor

While violas attract beneficial hoverflies and ladybugs, I grow them more for their color and edibility. They're like vibrant garden sprites, edging beds and spreading cheer.

Plant

SUN TO LIGHT SHADE. MODERATE TO REGULAR WATER.

Perennial grown as an annual. Prefers rich, well-draining soil. Grow from seed or starts. Direct-sow four to six weeks before your last spring frost and again in midsummer for a fall bloom. In warmer climates, it's possible to sow in late summer for a fall bloom or in fall for a spring bloom. Start indoors eight to 10 weeks before your last spring frost, or cast seeds in late fall to early winter. Bury seeds 1/8 inch deep. Seeds generally germinate best after chilly, wet weather, which they naturally receive when sown in fall. Violas are hardy and can overwinter down to USDA hardiness zone 4.

Plant along borders or as ground cover beneath taller plantings.

Pick

Harvest whole flowers as needed.

Fix

Remove stems and toss fresh flowers in salads, or candy them and add to cakes, cookies, popsicles or sorbet. Make floral-infused water by pairing flowers with citrus or cucumbers, or infuse them in vinegar.

More Companion Plants with Edible Flowers

Agastache. Add to cakes, syrups and beverages for an anise taste.

Arugula and other brassicas. Generally mild in flavor, they add wonderful color to salads and garnishes.

Basil. Wonderful in everything, the flowers of basil can be used as you would the leaves. They're especially good in salads or sprinkled over roasted vegetables.

Bee balm. Add these sweet and spicy flowers to jellies, salads, tea, rice or pasta.

Chamomile. This is a wonderful flower for a soothing tea.

Chives. Their mild onion flavor pairs perfectly with most savory foods and dressings.

Cilantro. Toss flowers over dishes as you would the leaves. Try them in tacos, on roasted veggies or with anything in need of something fresh.

Dill. Add dill flowers to pickles, scramble them with eggs, layer on fish, and sprinkle over potatoes and other veggies.

Fava, pea and green bean flowers. Mildly sweet and vibrant, these flowers make an everyday salad come to life.

Fennel. Make a fennel flower oil for braising or grilling; pair with fish, meats, greens or anything that could benefit from its natural licorice flavor.

Lavender. My favorite is lavender vanilla ice cream, but it's also lovely in soups and other savory dishes.

Lemon balm. Infuse in tea, add to dressings, or toss into roasted vegetables at the last minute.

Marjoram. Milder than oregano, it makes a lovely tisane or a fragrant addition to vegetables or fish.

Oregano. Use oregano flowers as you would the leaves. Sprinkle over pizza or pasta, mix into breads, or stir into butter or soups.

Rosemary. Use rosemary flowers as you would its leaves in savory pastries or breads, in dressings or sauces, or sprinkled over roasted vegetables or meats.

Roses. Brew into a tisane, make rose petal jam, or crystallize their petals to use in desserts.

Sage. These flowers are lovely with both summer and winter squash or when mixed into dressings, vinaigrettes or sauces.

Squash. Stuff squash blossoms with cheeses and vegetables, try them in quesadillas and pasta dishes, or add them to soups.

Thyme. Much like oregano, these flowers are a welcome addition to soups, breads, pasta dishes and dressings.

Candied Violets

It was renowned American botanist Luther Burbank who said, "Flowers always make people better, happier . . . they're sunshine, food and medicine for the soul." We're wired for flowers — to grow them, admire them, soak up their goodness and give them as gifts. When they find their way into a salad or a coating of sugar nestled on a cookie or atop a cake, something incredibly wonderful happens.

Makes 1 to 2 cups.

What You Need

Violets or other edible flowers

1 egg white

Superfine sugar you can easily make by running granulated sugar through a food processor or blender

Soft, fine-bristled paintbrushes

A spoon

Tweezers *optional

Parchment or wax paper

Baking pan or another surface for drying the flowers once sugared

What You Do

1. When I'm picking flowers I've grown myself (and I know they're organic and pesticide free), I don't bother washing them first. However, if you feel better washing your flowers before getting started, gently dip them in cool water, doing your best to keep the petals intact, or rinse them with a very light spray. Then, let them dry completely on a dish towel before moving to the next step.

2. Using a paint brush, gently coat the upper and under sides of one flower or flower petal at a time with egg white. Then, hold the flower over the sugar bowl and carefully spoon or sprinkle sugar onto the flower. (I find it's helpful to hold flowers by the nub of the stem, or try using tweezers.)

3. Place sugared flowers on parchment to dry for at least 12 hours. Once fully dry, use them right away, or store them in an airtight container between pieces of parchment or wax paper.

4. I've also had luck glazing flowers straight onto cookies and eating them on the spot. No drying or fussing needed. It's a one-step method that's also a kid favorite.

5. Use this same method with other edible flowers, such as rose petals and borage blooms.

Nasturtium Capers

My grandmother taught me that sometimes the best foods are the most unexpected. She used everything, from root to tip, whenever possible, and nasturtium seeds were no exception. If you can pickle a nasturtium seed, what can't you pickle?

When brined and pickled, nasturtium seeds become a peppery version of store-bought capers, which are actually the pickled flower buds of a shrub native to the Mediterranean.

To pickle nasturtium seeds, first gather them when they're still green. Before the seeds fall away from the plant, they can be found where the flowers once were, in a neat clump of three that should be separated out into individual seeds before pickling. You may also find bright green seed pods below plants — just steer clear of seeds that have begun to yellow and turn brown as they'll be tough and unpalatable.

Makes 1/2 pint. Double recipe as needed.

What You Need

3 tbsp. salt

1 1/2 cups water

2/3 cup nasturtium seed pods, separated and cleaned

3/4 cup white or white wine vinegar (5% acidity)

2 tsp. sugar

Sprig of thyme or a short sprig of rosemary

1 bay leaf

What You Do

BRINE SEED PODS

1. Combine salt and water in a saucepan and bring to a boil.
2. Put clean nasturtium pods into a quart-sized canning jar. Pour hot brine solution over seed pods, cover, and let soak for 2 or 3 days.
3. Once pods are brined for a couple of days, it's time to pickle them.

PICKLE

1. Drain and rinse the brine from the seed pods using a strainer, and place them in a half-pint jar.
2. Combine vinegar, sugar, herbs and bay leaf in a saucepan and bring to a boil.
3. Once boiling, let it simmer for a minute and stir to be sure sugar has dissolved.
4. Pour the vinegar mixture over nasturtium pods, making sure the herbs find their way into your jar. If you're making a double or triple batch, divide the herbs evenly between your jars and let cool.
5. Cover and refrigerate once jar reaches room temperature. Seeds are ready for eating after a few days in the fridge, but I like to let them sit for at least a week before adding them to dishes like roasted veggies, sautéed summer squash and salads. Store for up to six months for quick pickle batches, and eat within the year for best flavor if canning with a hot water bath.

At the end of the day, your feet should be dirty,
    your hair messy, and your eyes sparkling.
— SHANTI

the SIMPLE ACT
OF GROWING

GROW: SEEDING, PLANTING & PROPAGATING

One of the best things about any garden is that seeds, twigs and bits of roots are more than willing to grow into next season's crops. Many would volunteer if we let them, self-sowing and propagating, reminding us our job is to mimic nature as best we can. If we get the timing and techniques right, we will prune and gather our way to delicious somethings that find a way into our hearts and onto our tables.

SEED-SOWING BASICS

Have you ever looked inside a seed? If you open one up, you'll find a tiny plant. It's dormant, lying in wait with its leaves folded neatly together. You can just make out the root. Give it the right conditions — some warmth, water, light, air and a place to call home — and it will break dormancy and get to work, doing everything it can to reach the soil surface.

When giving plants their start, it helps to remember that they're not so different from you and me. They each have their own array of likes, dislikes, strengths, weaknesses — and quirks. There's no single rule to follow when it comes to helping them grow, just a set of guiding factors.

Direct-Sow or Transplant?

Direct-Sow

Direct-sow plants that tend to have a short growing season and are easy to grow. These plants aren't picky about soil, can tolerate colder temperatures, don't transplant well or have tap roots that develop best when sown directly.

Plants That Work

Carrots, beans, peas, beets, turnips, radishes, dill, cilantro, chervil, nasturtiums, borage, perpetual spinach, mizuna, edible red leaf amaranth, purslane

Transplant

Plan to start edibles inside if they have long growing seasons or take a considerable amount of time to germinate and develop.

Plants That Work

Tomatoes, basil, strawberries (*Fragaria vesca*)

Direct-Sow or Transplant

The flexibility to start some seeds indoors as well as out is incredibly helpful. If you're growing crops like lettuces, arugula and tatsoi successively and you're working with a small space, starting them in containers to transplant out later helps maximize garden beds and time.

Plants That Work

Lettuce, spinach, cucumbers, summer squash, parsley, arugula, kale, tatsoi, mâche, calendula, viola, radicchio, chives, Swiss chard

Warmth

Opposite, top: Beet sprout. Opposite, bottom: Planting snap peas, paper pots and all.

It's true that warmer temperatures speed germination; however, there are limits. Lettuces, for instance, won't germinate when temperatures rise above 85°F (29°C). Their ideal temperature range for germination is between 50 and 70°F (10 to 21°C), while summer squash will germinate when temperatures range from 60 to 105°F (16 to 41°C). Map out your frost dates, take note of monthly average temperatures, and compare your growing season with that of your plants (or plants to be). See page 15 for more on climate.

Water

Seeds need warmth paired with water to germinate. Give them just enough moisture so it's absorbed through the seed coat and stimulates and feeds growth. It's important to maintain an even amount of moisture until you see sprouts emerge. If soils dry out at any time, chances are it will interrupt the germination process and you'll have to start from scratch. That said, you also don't want overly soggy soil, which can cause seeds to drown and rot. When watering, a simple solution is to use a spray bottle or low-flow watering can to top-water, or better yet, water from the bottom by placing containers in a pan of water. This way water is naturally taken up by wicking as the soil surface dries out. (Just be sure to fill your watering pan every few days.)

Soil

Seeds aren't picky about soil fertility — they'll germinate even if the soil is poor. However, when direct-sowing it's smart to compost and amend garden beds before planting. This is your best shot at giving seedlings the nutrition they need at just the right moment.

When starting seeds in containers, the breakfast, lunch and dinner approach works well. Give them a light soil that's not necessarily nutrient rich when sowing (breakfast). This can be a basic potting soil, or a soilless mix or sterilized potting soil, which is especially helpful when growing tender varieties prone to damping-off, such as lettuces. Then, if potting up starts like tomatoes, plant them in a soil with more nutrition (lunch), such as a potting soil with some worm castings or compost tea thrown in. Dinner is served in the garden. It's the full meal deal including a helping of aged compost, composted manure or a fertilizer of your choice.

Damping-off

If newly emerged sprouts tip over, withering at the base of their stems, it's probably due to damping-off. Damping-off is a disease caused by fungi living in soil. It often occurs when seeds are overwatered or stressed because of overcrowding, or

if there's not enough light, warmth or circulation. One solution is to start seeds in sterile soil or a soilless mix, removing all chance of damping-off.

It's also possible to prevent damping-off by not overwatering, providing good air flow and beginning with clean, sterile containers. Other tricks I use to prevent damping-off include bottom-watering flats or paper pots and sprinkling vermiculite or a light layer of sand over just-planted seeds along with cinnamon (which acts as a natural fungicide).

Light

Most seeds don't require light to germinate. It's just the teeny seeds that are sown on top of the soil or close to the surface that need it. Seedlings, however, need lots of light. This is especially true of plants requiring full sun to grow. Once you see sprouts emerging from containers, place them in a bright, south-facing window or outside in a protected space like a cold frame, or supplement with artificial lights, giving them 15 hours per day. If seedlings become tall and leggy, it's a sign they need more light.

Make Your Own Seed-Starting Mix

It's easy to make your own seed-starting mix. This recipe is soilless, peat free and better than most anything you'll find at the store. Using peat moss in the garden is far from sustainable. (Did you know it can take 100 years or more for a peat bog to form?) Use coconut coir instead. It's a natural by-product of the coconut industry, has a neutral pH and possesses the same beneficial qualities as peat for holding moisture while improving drainage.

What You Need
8 parts hydrated coconut coir
3 parts worm castings
4 parts perlite or rice hulls

What You Do
Hydrate coir in a bucket of water for 30 minutes. Once it's flaky like compost, mix it with worm castings and perlite or rice hulls. Your final product should be light and crumbly. If it's too clumpy, add more perlite; if it's overly crumbly, add more coir.

Emily's Note

The first seeds I planted as a child were pumpkins and potatoes (they're easy for small hands to manage). I tucked them into the soil, copying my parents, and added my own quiet whisper before patting the soil nice and snug. It went something like this:
Dear Seed,
I love you. Please grow.
I can't wait to see you.
Emily

Presoaking Seeds

Two easy ways to pregerminate seeds are soaking them or placing them between a damp paper towel. A few hours of soaking can shorten the germination process by days, softening the seed coat and priming the seed for growth. I add a dash of liquid seaweed to water to give seeds an extra boost. Soak larger seeds overnight and smaller seeds, like carrots, for just an hour or two. Pregerminating bean seeds isn't recommended because it weakens their growth, but the rest are fair game.

Thinning

Seeds planted in rows or groups will most likely need thinning, although having a few too many is better than not enough. Thin in stages just in case you encounter a snail invasion or marauding birds. Have an idea of how big plants or roots will be at maturity, and thin to half this distance; then after a few weeks, thin again. Leave the sturdiest, most vigorous sprouts and take the smaller ones in between. Thin by pinching off or cutting seedlings with scissors as close to the ground as possible, and eat the tastiest sprouts as you go. In the final thinning, give plants enough room to grow to the size you hope to harvest.

Emily's Note

If seeds don't germinate, the soil could be too cold or hot, they could be buried too deeply, or they're being under- or overwatered. It could also be that the seeds simply weren't viable. Check your seed packet for an expiration date.

Hardening-off

Seedlings need time to get used to the outside world before moving from the indoors out to the garden, so it's best to help them acclimatize. The most common method is to take plants outside a week before transplanting and place them out of direct sun in a sheltered location for one or two hours, then bring them back inside. Take them out again the next day, and this time increase the time they spend outside by an hour. Continue this for at least a week, increasing the time by an hour each day. Skip days that are unseasonably cold or hot.

It's also possible to harden-off starts by placing them in a cold frame for two weeks before transplanting. A cold frame is like a mini greenhouse, but instead of having a door on the side, it's on the top and functions as a lid. Open the lid each day for increments similar to the first method: the first day for up to two hours, the second day for an hour longer, and so on.

WORKSHOP #4

HOW TO GROW PLANTS FROM SEED

1 Reuse yogurt containers, egg or milk cartons or paper cups — they all make excellent planters. You can also sterilize and replant in nursery pots and six packs, or make paper pots using newspaper and a small can (like a tomato paste can). They're biodegradable and can be planted directly in the garden.

2 Prepare your planting area or fill containers and moisten soil. (If soil is dry, it could take a day to fully hydrate.) Gently tamp and smooth the soil surface with your hand to ensure water won't pool or puddle and that seeds stay where you want them.

3 Seed size dictates how deep to sow — the larger the seed, the deeper it's sown. A measure commonly used is to bury seeds twice the depth of their diameter.

4 I sometimes use my finger or a pencil to make a furrow at the required depth for planting. Then, I fill it with seeds, sprinkling them in one at a time, giving each plenty of room to grow before covering them with soil. I push larger seeds, like beans or sunflowers, into the soil using my forefinger, and I scatter-sow smaller seeds, dropping them on the surface and covering them with a light layer of soil or vermiculite. (Seeds that need light aren't covered.) With all these methods, it's important to gently press the soil, ensuring seeds have good contact with their planting mix.

5 Overseeding can improve your chances for success, just be careful not to overdo it (thinning seedlings takes time). If working with small containers like paper pots, I sow one to three seeds per pot and pinch off the smaller seedlings once they emerge.

6 Label and date what you plant, or catalog your plantings on a calendar or in a journal. This allows you to track what you've grown and map successes and failures, which helps when selecting seeds the following season.

7 Water seeds using a misting bottle, a low-flow watering can or a micro-spray head connected to a drip system (best for direct-sowing), or by bottom-watering. Big splashes of water or a heavy flow can displace seeds, mix up soil and damage seedlings. Keep soil evenly moist — it should feel damp to the touch. Once seedlings emerge, let the soil surface dry out between waterings.

8 You can make a mini greenhouse over seedling containers to speed the germination process using a plastic bag or container. Just be sure to remove it once seeds sprout.

WORKSHOP #5
TRANSPLANTING

1 When potting up seedlings or moving them out to the garden, choose a cool, cloudy afternoon, or work in a sheltered location. Make sure the soil you're moving plants to is moist and ready to go.

2 Seeds sown together to conserve space need to be gently teased apart before potting up. It's best to do this when they've just developed their true leaves. Simply release them from their container and, using a pencil or chopstick, work their roots apart, disturbing the roots as little as possible. If you're working with plastic nursery pots, squeeze the side of the pot to loosen soil and release the plant without pulling on the plant stem. Tease apart the roots of root-bound plants, especially if they've taken on the shape of their container.

3 Move plants one at a time, holding them by their seed leaves. Make a depression in the soil of their new home that's big enough to hold their roots.

4 Tuck them in and lightly press the soil around the base of the stem to make sure starts are secure. Lightly pressing the soil eliminates air pockets and ensures water can wick without barriers throughout the soil and roots can move freely. It's important to not bury stems and to plant sprouts at the same depth they were originally growing.

5 Seeds sown in individual containers like paper pots can be potted up or transplanted out to the garden with little trouble. Dig or scoop a hole with a trowel or your hands that's the same size as the original container. With paper pots, I often peel away excess paper before submerging in soil. Then push soil back in around the plant, again making sure there are no air pockets or gaps in the soil that would hinder water movement or root development.

SUCCESSION PLANTING AND CUT-AND-COME-AGAIN CROPS

Plants with short life cycles like radishes, turnips, lettuces and cilantro can be planted multiple times throughout the growing season, ensuring a continuous harvest while maximizing space. This is known as succession planting or planting successionally. The length of time between seeding depends on the length of the plants' life cycle and the amount of available space in your garden. You may find you plant twice in a season or, as with radishes, which have a life cycle of about 30 days, every few weeks so you never go without.

Cut-and-come-again crops are plants that can be grown once and harvested several times, usually greens and other leafy edibles. Many tender herbs, like parsley and basil; the leaves of some root crops, like turnip greens; lettuces and amaranth can be grown to maturity and harvested, and some can be grown for baby leaves and sheared occasionally for small, tender greens.

HOW TO CHOOSE PLANTS AT THE NURSERY

Never buy a plant that looks diseased or compromised in any way. If you see black spots, strange mottling on leaves, curling of leaf edges or anything else that looks questionable, steer clear. There's a good chance plants with existing diseases won't grow to maturity, and they'll spread disease in your garden. Instead, look for plants that look lively, springy and in excellent health. If it looks happy it probably is, and this is the plant for you.

When purchasing six packs, look for containers that hold only one start per cell. This is especially important with plants like lettuces — they'll transplant far better than those that are overcrowded. The exception is if the starts are still very teeny and their true leaves have just developed. If this is the case, you'll want to pot them up as soon as you get home by pricking them out as when transplanting.

Plants to Grow from Cuttings, Divisions or Nursery Starts

Oregano/ Marjoram	Softwood cuttings in summer, or division in spring or after flowering
Thyme	Softwood cuttings in spring or summer, division, or layering in fall or spring
Rosemary	Softwood cuttings in spring or later summer, or layer decumbent varieties
Sage	Softwood cuttings in spring, or layer in spring
Cane berries	Softwood cuttings, division, or layering
Strawberries	Divide rooting stems (stolons)
Asparagus	Division in late winter or early spring
Rhubarb	Division fall to spring

WORKSHOP #6

ROOTING STEM CUTTINGS IN A SOILLESS MIX

Cut a 6-inch stem, measuring from the tip down and snipping below a leaf node or branching point. Exact measurements aren't necessary — just get it close. It's best to use a knife when cutting so plant tissue isn't compressed or squeezed together, as could happen with scissors.

If you're not planting your cutting right away, place it in water or wet a paper towel or newspaper and wrap it around the open end of the stem to keep it moist. Prepare a soilless mix. I like to use a 50/50 mix of perlite and vermiculite because they hold moisture while providing excellent drainage. You can substitute organic rice hulls for perlite (the hulls are more sustainable), or just use perlite or rice hulls, or make your own seed-starting mix. Some plants will grow in anything you put them in, including garden soil.

Remove the leaves from the bottom half of the stem. If you're using a rooting hormone, now is the time. After trying all sorts of rooting hormone products, I generally use liquid seaweed.

Press your cutting into your mixture until it's anchored, but avoid submerging it past the remaining leaves. Water it well and place it out of direct sunlight, but where the light is bright and the climate is warm.

It helps to make a mini greenhouse over your cuttings until they take root. Spritz them with a water bottle and then cover them with a plastic bag, using chopsticks or skewers for support. A plastic water bottle cut in half or recycled plastic containers also work well.

Check moisture levels every few days, and water only when the soil feels dry.

Roots will develop after about three or four weeks, depending on what you're growing. To check for root growth, I give the stem a gentle tug and if there's resistance, pot it up.

Grow more than one cutting at a time so you have extras to share, and experiment using this method with other plants (except woody shrubs and trees). Plant cuttings in your garden or in containers, just as you would transplants.

PROPAGATING PLANTS FROM CUTTINGS

The joints, leaf nodes, branching points and notches where stems connect to roots and roots connect to roots all have special tissue holding meristematic cells. These cells are considered undifferentiated, meaning they're designed to grow new plant parts of different kinds (leaves, roots, shoots, and so on), whatever the plant may need to continue thriving.

When growing plants from cuttings, take them at these nodes and branching points where it's possible for new roots to grow. To guarantee success, cuts are made just below nodes. Spring is an excellent time to begin the process, as plants are actively growing and putting on new growth — but if you have an opportunity to grow something new, take the chance while you have it (just avoid cuttings from plants that are dormant or in full bloom).

Rooting Stem Cuttings in Water

Pliable, soft-stemmed plants have the best chance of rooting in water. To root a cutting in water, clip 3 to 4 inches of a new shoot or stem, measuring from the tip down, just below the nearest branching point with a sharp knife or precision snips. Carefully remove the lower leaves, keeping a few growing near the tip, and place the cutting in a glass of water in bright light but out of direct sun. The trick is to change the water every day to prevent bacteria from building up. There's an inherent amount of success and failure when propagating plants, so take three or four cuttings and remember that not all plants can be propagated the same way. Herbs like oregano, thyme and sage won't root or don't perform as well as other plants using this method.

DIVIDING PLANTS

Divide when plants are past their peak growth season, using a spade. With herbs like thyme or chives, lift the entire plant (or as much of it as you can) out of the ground. Rinse the roots and shear back foliage to about 4 inches in height. Then, cut or separate plants into smaller clumps, leaving enough to form new growth. Plant them out or pot them up and water.

Rhubarb is divided in fall to spring when it's dormant and there are no leaves, but it's dug up in much the same manner as chives. Use a spade to work under the root system, loosening it as a whole. It's easy to see where buds have formed in preparation for next season's growth. Carefully cut the root so there's at least one main bud per chunk. Replant the individual chunks, giving them plenty of room to grow, and amend with aged manure.

TENDING & TRAINING

The job of deciding what to grow is done. Planting is done (at least for now). This is the time when I find myself stealing looks at what's taking root as though, if I stop and stare long enough, I'll witness the act of growing first-hand. And somehow I always do, although it happens in a collection of moments and over the course of days.

GARDENING BASICS

I sometimes think that tending a garden once it's in place is where the love affair begins. It's the time when bonds are forged and rewards are realized. Sure, some plants die while others thrive, and mistakes happen, but that's all part of it. The process of staking, watering, inspecting and weeding will eventually lead to harvesting, and in the meantime, there are flowers.

SMART WATERING

How much water is enough? Touch the soil and look and feel under the soil surface. If it looks wet or feels wet, then you're likely in good shape. If it's dry an inch or more down, it may be time to water. Plants are also good at telling us when they're thirsty by how they appear, taste or react to their environments. In general, when plants don't get enough water, they become stressed, leaf tips may burn and turn brown, they're prone to disease, growth is stunted, and fruit and leaf development is poor. Leaves may also feel dry and crackly, while the leaves of lettuces and other leafy greens become tough and bitter — plus they're more likely to bolt.

Too much water can lead to similar symptoms. Plant roots may rot or starve from lack of oxygen, causing leaves to wilt, turn yellow or drop, even when soil feels damp to the touch. Above all, fruit loses its flavor. And those cracks you sometimes see on tomatoes? They're caused by inconsistent watering.

The Best Way to Water Plants

What's below is also above. In order for lush, beautiful plants to grow above the ground, they need to develop lush, beautiful roots below it. Water with the root zone in mind. Are you growing seedlings or lettuces with shallow root systems, or tomatoes, whose roots run deep?

Water deeply using the slowest delivery system possible. This will wet the entire root zone from top to bottom and beyond, encouraging roots to explore. The healthier the root system, the healthier your plants.

Give plants water when they need it. Weather, climate and season affect the amount and timing of watering, along with wind, sun and humidity. It can change from one day to the next. Keep an eye on plants, and check soil moisture by pushing a finger underground or taking a look (without disturbing roots). In general, if soil is dry an inch or more down, water. This varies from plant to plant. Drought-tolerant plants like rosemary prefer soil to dry out between watering, while tender herbs such as cilantro tip over when soils aren't kept reasonably moist.

Morning is the best time to water. This gives plants time to dry out before the sun drops, decreasing the spread of waterborne diseases like leaf spot or blights. It also helps manage slug and snail populations. That said, if plants are wilting or look stressed from intense heat, give them water no matter the time of day. Shading certain plants such as greens may also be necessary.

Cover crops, interplanting and mulch all keep soil moisture from evaporating. Apply mulch or coarse compost to cover bare soil, and interplant by pairing taller and shorter plants. Grow edible flowers or other companion plants to reduce the amount of bare soil. (See page 244 on interplanting.)

Water at soil level. If you can set up a drip or soaker hose system, do it before you plant. Not only would all my plants die if relegated to hand-watering (because I don't have the patience for it), but it's also not the best delivery system. Have a hose with an adjustable nozzle or wand handy, of course, but save it for emergency watering. If you must use a sprinkler, remember to water in the morning for best results and the least amount of evaporation.

When to Hand-Water

I have some longtime gardening friends who swear by hand-watering. They say it's the only way to really get to know your plants. You just need to consider the time involved, how plants are watered when you travel and how to water plants like tomatoes that prefer water delivered at soil level. Direct-sown seeds and seedlings also benefit from light hand-watering (see page 218), as do plants that are stressed or wilting due to intense sun.

Watering Systems

A well-planned **drip or soaker hose system** with an irrigation timer takes the worry out of gardening and reduces your time commitment. There are simple setups that connect to a spigot and can be run along decks or patios, and more elaborate systems for larger gardens. Once they're in, they're easy to care for and modify as needed, whether you're adding micro-spray heads for seedlings, single-stream heads for planters or a drip line for beds.

An **olla** is an unglazed, low-fired clay vessel that's buried underground near plant root zones. Water wicks through the walls of the pot and into soil as it dries out, naturally delivering water as it's needed. Fill them from the top every few days and that's it. They're especially handy when gardening in larger planters.

Top: Water at the root zone by placing ollas in containers. Middle: Make your own nanny pot with up-cycled bottles. Bottom: Old pans are perfect for bottom watering seedlings.

I use **nanny pots** to water planters and other small containers that I would otherwise hand-water. If you're away for a long weekend or simply want to guarantee plants are getting the water they need, fill a bottle with water, flip it over, and push the open end into the soil. The soil will seal the opening, and as with an olla, water will flow from the bottle as the soil dries out.

Self-watering containers operate on a similar principle to ollas, wicking water held in storage into soil. You can make your own or buy them ready made.

Bottom-watering systems are my method of choice when it comes to watering seeds, seedlings and newly potted up transplants. Place seedling pots or flats in a pan of water, and water will wick up through the soil.

STAKING AND TRELLISING

It's best to stake and trellis climbing and top-heavy crops when they're planted. Pole beans, runner beans, cucumbers and summer squash all benefit from trellising. Though cucumbers and summer squash don't require it, growing them up instead of out maximizes square footage, improves circulation and increases sun exposure.

A trellis is any sort of framework that supports climbing plants and gives them something to hold on to. Make one with bamboo, recycled wood, chicken or hog wire and jute twine. Repurpose and customize an existing fence, or create a simple structure you can use year after year, such as a teepee or an arbor. Tomatoes simply need something to keep them upright. Staking works well, although I often use cages when I plan to be away for extended periods at the beginning of the growing season.

PRUNING, DEADHEADING AND TIDYING UP

If a plant looks scraggly or is becoming gangly and overgrown, as is common with rosemary, it's time to clean it up. Often the old, dead leaves of plants like strawberries and violas come free on their own when you comb through them with your hands. However, there are others that benefit from pruning or deadheading, both of which stimulate growth and give fresh life to plants.

Clip spent flowers either below the bud or just above the node directly below the flower when deadheading. Deadhead violas, calendula, scented geranium and other flowers for continued blooms. Because violas are so tiny, it's best to shear them with snips or pinch or brush off old flowers with your hands. Use clippers or scissors for larger blooms, and leave some flowers in place for seed saving or as fodder for birds.

Methods for pruning are plant specific. Perennials like oregano and thyme and sages like pineapple sage benefit from annual shearing or pruning to nearly the ground between life cycles (after flowering and before new growth begins to set). You can grow more basil this way too, though instead of shearing to the ground, simply take stems of leaves down to the second or third node (see page 54). With woody shrubs like blueberries and small, container-grown fruit trees, prune just above nodes to manipulate plant shape, reduce cross-branching and improve air circulation. However, get to know your plants before cutting. The timing of pruning and what is pruned will affect the life of the plant and future harvests.

Weeding

Weeds will fill beds and planters regardless of the measures taken to prevent them. But just because you didn't plant them doesn't mean they don't have value. Many are edible and highly nutritious, like purslane; some offer food and habitat to beneficial insects; and others can be added to hot compost. However, weeds can easily outcompete the plants you've taken so much care to grow.

Gardening in planters and raised beds immediately makes the job of weeding easier, allowing you to target your attention on a defined space. Apply mulch and interplant whenever possible to cover the ground, making it difficult for weeds to take hold, and spend a few minutes each week pulling them up when they're tiny, before they set deep roots or their flowers have gone to seed. I generally hand-weed or use a trowel or tiller mattock where grasses and other tough customers have taken hold in large areas.

As a child, sitting still and pulling plants from the ground was torture. Somewhere over the years, that changed. There's something truly wonderful about looking

through plants, brushing past some to get to others, and learning to identify what stays and what goes. You get to know your plants up close and personal. You'll discover some of your most-loved edibles have self-seeded, volunteering a fresh crop without your help. Look for sunflowers, calendula, dill and strawberries in spring. Maybe purslane will be among the group, and if so, prop it up and prepare to add it to summer salads.

FEED YOUR GARDEN

Just like people, plants need a steady supply of nutrition to flourish. Start with the healthiest soil possible and add amendments to boost fertility throughout the growing season. Leaf mold, compost, aged manure, worm castings, seaweed and manure tea all work well. Store-bought granular fertilizers are fine, too. Whatever you decide to use, make sure it's organic, chemical free and not synthetic, and keep the process as simple as possible.

I apply a modest layer of aged manure to planting beds and top it with a 2-inch layer of organic compost in spring and fall. Leaf mold and coarse compost work well for the top layer, doubling as a mulch. Potted plants and other small-container gardens get a fresh batch of soil in spring and then layers of manure and compost. I toss in fresh compost when planting so it's near the root zone, and then as plants grow, I make manure tea to fertilize every two or three weeks throughout the growing season. New transplants are watered with liquid seaweed to aid in root development and later get an occasional foliar feeding of liquid seaweed with a spray bottle.

Container-grown plants exist in small ecosystems. They need to be watered and fertilized frequently because of increased leaching and the fact that there are fewer resources available in a smaller space. Soil within small containers quickly becomes dense, so liquid fertilizers like manure tea, worm tea and seaweed extract are essential.

Emily's Note

The Organic Materials Review Institute (OMRI) is an international nonprofit organization that tests and reviews products for organic use. Look for a list of OMRI-certified products or the OMRI stamp of approval on products before you buy.

The goal is to give plants amendments they recognize and easily assimilate, which in nature come from other plants and animals. This is why leaves, compost and manure are central to an organic system. Of the major nutrients needed by plants, nitrogen is one of the hardest to secure and the quickest to be consumed. Manures are excellent for replacing nitrogen. The key is to use aged or composted manure, as fresh manure will burn plants. Plants also absorb nutrients through their leaves and stems, which is where kelp and other foliar sprays come in.

Mulch

Mulch is one of the best gifts you can give your garden, no matter the size.

- A layer of mulch over soil acts like a blanket, keeping soil cool in summer when temperatures rise and warm as temperatures drop.

- It provides a protective barrier, making it harder for weeds to plant themselves, while protecting and improving soil moisture and structure.

- Mulch supplies continuous organic matter to soil, much like leaves as they fall to the forest floor.

🐦 Splashing of water from soil to plant leaves is eliminated when mulch is present, reducing the spread of water- and soil-borne diseases.

🐦 Straw, compost, leaves, bark, wood chips and even shredded newspaper can be used to mulch beds. Look for mulch that is local, and reuse leaves and other organic materials found in your yard or community.

🐦 The amount of mulch you use depends on the material. Straw is light and bulky, so a 4-inch layer works well because it packs down with time. If you're using bark or wood chips around berries, for instance, an inch is enough, whereas a 2- to 3-inch layer of compost works well, especially at the start of the season. Just be careful as too much mulch (5 to 6 inches or more) can reduce circulation, hold too much moisture and spread disease.

GARDENING IN WINTER

It's possible to garden year round with the right materials, equipment or growing season. In the coldest of climates, plants need to go into the ground in summer to late summer so they can grow to near maturity before chilling temperatures set in. Some crops can be harvested from under the cover of snow, given the right protection, while others hunker down and continue to grow later as weather warms, providing an early spring harvest.

It may sound like a lot of work, but I can't think of a single cool-season veggie that doesn't improve with flavor thanks to cold. Carrots, kale, mustards, turnips and other brassicas all have heightened flavor after frost because the cold causes starches to convert to sugars, preventing plants from freezing.

Extend the Growing Season

Cold frames, hoop houses, cloches, greenhouses, row covers (horticultural fleece) and mulch are all excellent season extenders, protecting plants and helping each of us buy a little more time on either end of our frost dates. It's also possible to grow many tender herbs and greens indoors when given enough sun. The key to extending the season is to find a method that traps and protects heat in soil and air. Some intensify sun, while others filter it, but the end goal of amplifying heat is the same.

Make a **hoop house** with 1/2- to 1-inch flexible tubing or metal wire. Cut pieces to fit the width of planters or beds, giving plenty of head room for growing plants. Fix either end into soil or fit them over stakes, making sure they're well anchored. The hoops then provide support for your material of choice: plastic, row covers or netting to defend against roving birds.

Cloches are an excellent solution if you have only a handful of plants to protect. I've seen entire gardens covered with cloches, all made from recycled plastic milk jugs with their tops cut off, each one acting like a mini greenhouse. Glass or plastic bowls also work well as upcycled cloches, or buy glass cloches made just for the job of protecting plants.

Cold frames and greenhouses can be made from recycled materials (a cold frame is the more economical of the two). A cold frame is a box with a lid that allows light to pass through. Make one with wood, repurpose old bricks, or employ straw bales as the sides or walls. An old window or a thick piece of plastic works well. Place it in a sunny location or near the radiant heat of a building, or modify an existing raised bed.

Floating row covers can be placed directly over plants or suspended by hoops or other structures. Lightweight covers elevate temperatures by about 4°F (2.2°C) and are great for protecting plants from pests and light frost. Midweight covers elevate temperatures by 6°F (3.3°C), while heavyweight covers elevate temperatures by about 8°F (4.4°C). The heavier the cover, the more light is blocked, so plants will grow more slowly. Plastic covers can also be used, elevating temperatures by 30°F (16.5°C) or more — be careful to provide ventilation and to elevate plastic covers using a hoop system. Attach row or plastic covers to hoops with clothespins or clips, and anchor them to the soil with rocks.

FOLLOW NATURE, HARVEST & CONTINUE GROWING

The secret to growing more in less space is to follow nature. If you look closely at any healthy living system, you'll find diversity: plants of different kinds rubbing shoulders, good bugs and bad, a variety of birds and likely a crowd of creatures you don't recognize — but they're part of the puzzle too. When we design a garden as a slice of life, the rewards go beyond a coveted bouquet of basil or a colander of tomatoes. You'll discover that you benefit from this touchpoint with nature as much as the plants you're growing, and you'll have a greater variety of flavorful and robust ingredients to work with in the kitchen.

ADD DIVERSITY TO YOUR GARDEN

I love neat rows of veggies as much as the next person. There's something wonderful about seeing them, knowing everything has its place. But by letting go a little and embracing what feels like chaos, planting with diversity in mind improves plants' ability to work together, reducing the need to rotate crops or counterattack pests. It doesn't mean you need to give up row planting altogether, but it gives you room for different crops to share space — often called interplanting, intercropping or planting a polyculture instead of a monoculture. This is also where companion planting comes into play, which is always a wonderful excuse to grow flowers.

Interplanting

Interplanting is a technique for growing plants with different maturation times or growth habits beside one another to increase yields from what is essentially the same amount of space. Why not plant quick-growing radishes next to carrots, or lettuces next to tomatoes? The radishes will be out long before the carrots are ready, and they'll remind you where the slower-germinating carrots are planted. Meanwhile, lettuces benefit from the shade offered by tomatoes in midsummer, and their shallow roots don't interfere with the deeper root systems set by tomatoes.

Interplanting also covers ground with plants you want to grow instead of weeds, aids with pest management and naturally decreases disease buildup in soil that's associated with growing a single crop from season to season. Try growing a mix of plants to simply confuse pests, making it harder and less likely for them to find their preferred targets. Or grow trap crops, which are plants that lure pests away from one plant to another. Nasturtiums are good for this because aphids love nasturtiums. Give the flowers a spot in a corner or at the edge of a bed away from other prized edibles, and hope the bugs take the bribe. Other highly fragrant, even pungent, plants like chives are also great at deterring pests.

Companion Planting

There are plenty of theories out there as to which plants like each other and which plants don't. Some say carrots love tomatoes but should never be planted with dill or cilantro. Or that beets and mustards should never be grown side by side. I almost always pair tomatoes and basil because basil improves the flavor of tomatoes (or so I've found), and I find interplanting with onions and calendulas helpful because the scent of onions confuses carrot flies and deters aphids, while calendulas are wonderfully attractive to pollinators.

It's also possible to pair plants much like with interplanting, where taller plants such as sunflowers are grown next to pole beans so there's no need for a trellis (the pole beans climb the sunflowers as they grow). In turn, beans fix nitrogen in soil, replenishing supplies from one growing season to the next. Grow summer squash at their feet, and now you have a trio of helpers. The squash will cover the ground, keeping weeds at bay, and decrease moisture loss from the soil.

HOW TO COMBINE PLANTS

Start with a handful of plants from the plant directory — whatever's on your "love this, must grow" list. Consider your space and possible companion plants, then devise a plan. How can you create a riot of color, a buzzing of bees and a hotbed of flavor all in one spot?

Combine shorter plants with taller ones. Place shorter, sun-loving plants on the south side of taller plants and shorter plants that require some shade on the north or east side of taller ones.

Place edibles with shallow root systems (like lettuces and tender herbs) near plants with deep-running roots (tomatoes and chard), and grow quick-growing crops (radishes, cilantro and little finger carrots) between those with longer growing seasons (sunflowers and pole beans).

Pair flowering herbs, nasturtiums and other edible flowers with fruits and veggies. They'll attract pollinators and provide fragrance to mix up the scents (confusing pests that find their targets via smell).

EASY SOLUTIONS FOR SUMMER COMPANION PLANTING

1 Grow veggies that need part shade (lettuces, chard, chervil, cilantro, parsley) to the north of taller plants (sunflowers, pole beans, dill, tomatoes). Let spring edibles (rhubarb, asparagus, mizuna, tatsoi, spring onions) get a head start before summer edibles gain height.

2 Strategically place taller, shade-producing plants (sunflowers, pole beans, dill, tomatoes) toward the north end of your garden. Interplant with radishes and other quick-growing crops.

3 Let summer squash and cucumbers trail at the feet of taller veggies (pole beans, sunflowers) to optimize space, cover ground and prevent weed growth. Tuck edible flowers and herbs along borders (borage, oregano).

4 Grow sun-loving plants to the south (radicchios, basil, oregano, thyme, sage, borage, red leaf amaranth).

5 Place edible flowers, herbs and trailing plants along borders (calendula, violas, thyme, nasturtiums).

ORGANIC GARDENING

There's no need to use chemicals in your kitchen garden to protect plants from pests and disease when you can grow organically. Pesticides and synthetic fertilizers are haphazard and indiscriminate. They're harmful not just to the pests and diseases in your garden but also to your food, to you, to me and beyond. Many linger in soil and have long-lasting, compounding effects, poisoning water and the places we call home. Organic practices are enough, especially when you take a simple, systematic approach and check on your garden as often as possible. Growing a handful of beneficial plants, following a few basic tenets and taking a quick stroll with your morning tea to keep an eye on things is all you need to do to ward off unwelcome guests.

What You Should Know Before Planting

- Grow flowers with veggies.

- Cultivate soil. Robust soil life is the foundation for robust plant life.

- Choose plant varieties best suited to your climate and growing season and that are also resistant to pests common to your region. For instance, you may love summer squash, but if you live in a cool coastal climate, you'll find you're constantly battling diseases like powdery mildew. Summer heat will draw aphids to kale, so grow perpetual spinach and edible amaranth when temperatures rise. If carrot flies are a problem, look for resistant varieties.

- Plant intensively to maximize space, but be careful to give plants enough room to breathe. Adequate air circulation is key to warding off disease.

- Mulch with compost to decrease the chance of soil-borne diseases, such as early blight and Septoria leaf spot, splashing up onto leaves.

- Water at ground level whenever possible to minimize the chance of blights and leaf spot.

- Keep your garden tidy. Clear away dead plant material and leaves that could harbor pests and disease.

- Clean tools and reusable seedling containers between use.

- Keep your garden well weeded. Weeds are an easy home for diseases and pests. Plant companion plants and other edibles strategically to prevent weeds from cropping up.

- Learn your friends. Pollinators and beneficial insects are on your side.

GOOD BUGS AND BAD BUGS

Good bugs are beneficial insects such as pollinators and bugs that eat other bugs. Some of them you know, like ladybugs and honeybees, while others do their work with fewer accolades, like spiders.

Bad bugs are those herbaceous critters that feast on our plants, sucking fluids from stems, chewing leaves, spreading disease and making homes in all the places we'd rather they didn't. That said, a healthy system has a mix of both, and quite honestly, some bugs cross the line and truly are both, reminding us that wonderful things can come from welcoming a mix of the two.

Butterflies, such as the anise swallowtail, lay their eggs on host plants like dill, fennel and parsley. These eggs then hatch into caterpillars, which eat the host plants in the process of becoming adult butterflies. Harvesting dill and other leaves with holes chewed in them won't hurt you. However, in some cases, like with cabbage white butterflies, the work of the larvae can decimate entire crops, sometimes overnight. It's a good idea to get to know your most common garden visitors and whether you should welcome their company.

Common Beneficial Insects

Attract pollinators with flowers.

Bees and butterflies. Honeybees, bumblebees, native bees and butterflies are all important pollinators.

Dragonflies. Adult dragonflies and damselflies eat gnats, mosquitos and midges.

Ground beetles. Ground beetles of all kinds prey on cutworms, cabbage root maggots, aphids and slug and snail eggs.

Hoverflies, or syrphid flies. Adults are important pollinators, and hoverfly larvae eat aphids, thrips and other plant-eating insects.

Lacewings. The larvae of lacewings look a little like tiny alligators that prey on aphids, spider mites, thrips, mealybugs and scale insects. (They're sometimes called "aphid lions.")

Ladybugs. Both adults and larvae eat aphids as well as whiteflies, mites and scale insects.

Parasitic wasps. Adult parasitic wasps lay their eggs inside the larvae of host insects, which die when the wasps reach maturity.

Common Pests

Aphids. Look for winged and wingless aphids congregating in clusters on plants. If you see ants, aphids could be close by, as ants often feed on the honeydew of aphids (the sugars excreted from eating plants). To control, wash plants with a heavy spray of water, apply soapy water (or horticultural soap) repeatedly until populations diminish, and employ ladybugs and other aphid-loving insects. To encourage beneficial insects to stay, give them a home with mulch and low-lying herbs like oregano, plant flowers with pollen they love (like calendula, scented geranium and dill) and don't use pesticides.

Cabbage worms. Look for cabbage worms on the leaves of kale and other brassicas like mustards. They often eat leaves from the outside in, leaving large, irregular holes. To control, handpick and apply Bt.

Top: Aphids love these fava beans — a little too much! Bottom: Handpicking cabbage worms.

Carrot flies. Carrot flies find their targets through smell and are also attracted to parsnips, celery and parsley. You'll know your plants are infested when the greens turn yellowy bronze and the roots have blackish runnels and scars. To prevent, avoid thinning by sowing carefully and with adequate spacing. If you do thin carrots, do so on a cloudy day when the smell of the thinnings is less volatile. Plant carrots near chives, or interplant with other fragrant plants to confuse carrot flies. It also helps to grow carrots in containers or beds elevated 2 feet or more off the ground.

Caterpillars. Caterpillars are herbaceous, requiring a host plant to feast on until maturity. Before removing, do your best to figure out what the caterpillar will be when it's an adult. (It may be a butterfly you'd like to encourage in your garden.) To control, handpick and discard, encourage predators and employ floating row covers if the problem persists.

Cutworms. Cutworms are most active in May and June. You'll know they're in the soil when you find the stems of small plants chewed at ground level. To control, handpick them at night, put protective collars around transplant stems or use Bt.

Potato beetles. If your tomatoes are losing leaves, potato beetles could be the culprit. Your best line of defense is to place a thick layer of straw mulch beneath plants, pick the beetles off plants by hand and attract beneficial insects.

If you're not sure what's eating your garden, look for signs of animals like these snail trails.

Slugs and snails. Slugs and snails are pernicious creatures. They love damp environments, tender new seedlings and fresh, young fruit, like ripening strawberries — basically all a thriving garden has to offer. It's best to expect they'll make your home theirs and to take a holistic approach to managing them.

If possible, use a drip system for watering and limit top-down spraying, especially in the second half of the day. This reduces moisture on the soil surface, making it less hospitable for slugs. If you have a known slug problem, start seeds in containers and plant them out only once they're big enough to fend for themselves. Next, if you were a slug, where would you hide? Look under things: dense grasses, weeds, rocks, fence railings and anything else providing cover. Slugs are also very good at using the edges of garden beds, where pockets naturally occur, sneaking just under the soil surface.

Be prepared to handpick slugs and snails and discard them. If you can't stand smooshing them, they're excellent chicken food. If you don't have chickens, find a friend or school garden that does.

Barriers are effective. If it's not raining a ton, I ring newly planted areas, sprouting peas and other tender plants with diatomaceous earth. I've tried using copper tape but without much success. However, crushed eggshells, coffee grounds and sawdust have proven handy, especially when sprinkled over soil that's just been seeded.

A beer trap is always a winner. Make one out of any shallow container, filling it about halfway. I often use empty mint tins, but container lids and shallow dishes also work well. Place the traps on top of the soil, pushing them in a bit to anchor them, and see what you've caught the next morning. Refill the traps with fresh beer every few days until the problem subsides or your plants have grown.

Squash bugs. These pests love squash and cucumbers. Look for squash bugs in groups on leaves, stems and fruit. To control, choose varieties resistant to squash bugs, handpick and discard, place floating row covers over immature plants and dust diatomaceous earth over infected areas.

Tomato hornworms. Large but difficult to spot, these caterpillars are voracious eaters of tomato, pepper and potato plants. To control, handpick and place in soapy water, or use predatory insects or Bt.

Whiteflies. Commonly found on the underside of leaves, these pests make a white cloud of flying insects when disturbed. To control, wash plants with a hard stream of water, spray with soapy water, employ lacewings and use sticky traps to catch them.

Tomato hornworm.

ANIMALS IN THE GARDEN

Cats, rabbits, foraging birds, deer, gophers, voles — they love your garden as much as you do. The best solution for keeping them out are barriers. However, the barriers differ a little from one animal to the next based on their particular habits, so figure out who your visitors are and block them accordingly.

- Gophers and voles make their homes in the ground and tunnel through soil, making in-ground plantings an easy target. Gopher baskets work well for individual plantings, and raised beds lined with gopher wire or 1/4-inch hardware cloth are a sure bet for keeping gophers out because they don't climb. But voles do. With voles, you'll need additional barriers in beds along with a plan for trapping them. It's not pretty, but I've found surrounding plants or entire beds with a wall of fine-mesh wire works best.

- Most cats aren't too troublesome, except cat poop in garden planters and veggie beds is gross and carries teratogens, a toxic substance known to cause birth defects. Reduce bare ground by planting intensively and utilizing ground covers. Place a cross-hatching of wood slats between plants and mulch beds. If you have a real problem, set up a motion-sensitive sprayer. Always dig out poop and place coffee grounds and other strong-smelling compost in its place so you don't get a repeat customer.

- Fence off deer and rabbits. With rabbits, drive the fencing underground by at least a foot, and create an L so it goes down and then out and away from the fence. (This also works well for voles and gophers.)

- As an added barrier, try planting a dense ring of narcissus (daffodil) bulbs outside the fencing. Daffodils are toxic, and animals generally don't like burrowing under them, although more than once I've found them moved after winter by squirrels — so think of them as a deterrent rather than a divisive barrier.

- I find foraging birds are seasonal. They come looking for young, tender seedlings, sometimes in spring and often in fall. You'll know they've been visiting if you find nubs of sprouts with no leaves — and they can work fast, sometimes clearing out a planting in less than an hour. If you suspect they'll come, save frustration by using hoops and netting to cover beds.

CONTINUE GROWING

The season has shifted, the carrots are long gone from the ground and all the beans are picked, but the chard is hanging on strong, and if you're lucky, the birds will leave a few sunflower seeds for next season's planting. With herbs to gather and store, pesto and preserves to make and a full sweep of tidying at hand, the changing weather ignites action. I hanker for these days as much as for those of midseason when the garden almost runs itself. It reminds me that the seasons of the year are my seasons too, marking time and offering up a joy that comes from small, good things — a batch of jam neatly stored, herbs waiting for the first pot of winter soup and canned tomatoes ready to brighten many meals in the coming months.

WORKSHOP #8

FOUR EASY WAYS TO PRESERVE HERBS

1 **Air-dry** leafy herbs like oregano, basil, sage, rosemary and thyme. The key to air-drying is a warm environment with good ventilation, and to keep cuttings out of direct sun. Start by shaking away loose dirt, pulling off any yellow and withered leaves, and returning hitchhiking bugs to the garden. You can also wash your trimmings and run them through a salad spinner or towel them dry. Spread clean herbs with larger leaves on a flat, coarsely woven drying basket so they're in a single layer, or hang them to dry. When hang-drying, bundle stems together with twine or a rubber band, and suspend them upside down. If you're worried about losing leaves to gravity, tuck a paper bag or muslin cloth around plants to catch leaves and flowers before they fall (just be sure there's room for air to move so moisture can escape). Once herbs are completely dry and brittle to the touch, place them in jars or airtight bags. It's best to use them within a year.

2 **Oven-drying** herbs is faster than air-drying, and if it's especially humid, it may be necessary to oven-dry herbs to prevent them from molding. Spread herbs on a baking sheet lined with parchment, turn your oven to 150°F and leave the door ajar. Check periodically and remove them once they feel crisp and dry. (This should take one to four hours, depending on the plants and your oven.)

3 **Food dehydrators** provide just the right amount of heat, and a built-in fan forces air in and around plants, eliminating the chance of mold and speeding up the process. They're especially nice for thicker, more succulent leaves. Simply place stems in single layers on individual racks, close the dehydrator and check on them periodically. Once leaves are crumbly, they're ready to be stored.

4 **Freezing** herbs in oil or butter is one of the best ways to retain their vibrant, fresh flavors. (The flavors we taste in herbs are actually aromatic oils, which are best preserved in — you guessed it — oil!) Wash and dry herbs by rinsing or soaking leaves and flowers in water, and then spin them in a salad spinner. Next, chop them up as you would when cooking, or use a food processor. Combine 1/3 cup olive oil for every 2 cups of leaves, or if using butter, combine 1/2 cup butter for every 2 cups of leaves. Blend the mixture, then freeze it flat in sheets so it's easy to break when you need some. You can also pour the mixture into ice cube trays. When freezing the mixture flat, I like to pour it over parchment on a cookie sheet, place it in the freezer until it's solid, then break it into chunks and store in an airtight container.

Making jam

Blackberry jam

For the winter

SAVORING YOUR HARVEST

It's hard to imagine growing too much basil or more tomatoes than you can eat, but it happens — and it's often in your favor. A glut means pickles, an opportunity to experiment with new preserves and plenty of herbs for drying. However, sometimes changing weather forces a quick harvest when you're least prepared. This is when freezer space comes in handy, dehydrators and old-fashioned drying methods can seem like a miracle, and a fermenting crock produces the next best thing to fresh.

When faced with a glut, start with what you know, then experiment. As a child, I watched my mom peel and chop boxes of apples, spice them with cinnamon and divvy them up (8 cups per freezer bag) to make pies through the winter. Berries were gently washed, dried and spread out on a cookie sheet, then popped in the freezer. Once the berries were firm, we combined them into larger containers where they were kept frozen until there was time to make jam, pies and ice cream. Now I do these things too.

It was later that I added drying and dehydrating to my fall to-do list and discovered the beauty of pickling and making pesto and salsa. It's true, basil makes fabulous pesto, but so do any number of greens, herbs and weedy things. And who says pickles must be made with cucumbers? The best "pickles" often end up being a mix-and-match medley from the garden.

PLANNING NEXT SEASON'S GARDEN

Bumper crops and failures are your roadmap for what to plant in the coming season. What came up short, and what can you do without? Do you wish you had more beets for pickling, or did you find yourself rummaging around in the garden in hopes of unearthing a turnip you might have missed? Adjust your planting list accordingly. If weather favored 'Sungold' tomatoes while none of the 'Black Krim' ripened, it may not be time to give up altogether on your favorite heirloom, but it's something to note for next season.

Saving Seeds

The trick to saving seeds is to store them well away from the conditions required for them to break dormancy and germinate: moisture, heat, light and air. Make sure seeds are fully dry, then tuck them into envelopes, label them, and store them in airtight jars and other containers. Place the envelopes in a cool, dark corner of your basement, a closet or a refrigerator. If humidity is a concern, tie 2 tbsp. dehydrated milk in a tissue and place it in with your seeds to absorb and hold excess moisture.

When collecting seeds of heirloom and open-pollinated varieties like calendulas, sunflowers and cucamelons, I always sprinkle a few in the garden where I'd like them to pop up next season. I find the plants that self-sow do so at just the right time and produce some of the hardiest plants, and all except those with taproots can be moved around the garden the following season.

Seeds saved from one season to the next gradually adapt to your unique micro-climate. They're far more likely to thrive, even when conditions seem unfavorable, and when you save seeds from season to season, you need to buy them only once — which is true of both open-pollinated and heirloom seeds. (It's best not to save the seeds of hybrid varieties like 'Sungold' and 'Early Girl' tomatoes and instead purchase them each year to guarantee flavor and vigor.)

PASS IT ON

Every year I find room to grow something new. Just a few seasons ago it was cucamelons; last year it was scented geranium. (Both of which made me wonder why I hadn't grown them before.) Your garden is the perfect place to let this process unfold. It gives you room to play and room to experience your food in a whole new way. You'll begin to understand plants from the inside out, and with the work and effort you've dedicated to your garden, joy grows — a joy that is deeply satisfying, like neat rows of vegetables, making you feel as though all is right with the world. This is the difference a garden can make in your life, and best of all, you can grow it yourself.

Collectively, the patchwork of our gardens comes together like a great big hug. They nourish our lives and our families, and they nourish our communities. Continued development and declining bee and butterfly populations remind us that what we plant and grow, along with the food choices we make, can have a significant impact on the world around us.

Fortunately, there are endless ways to continue growing. Trying new varieties is one, as is documenting your garden, keeping track of the seasonal foods you found especially inviting. Take photos and keep a journal.

You can include friends and neighbors by sharing seeds, hosting a veggie swap (especially in mid to late summer), exchanging recipes and finding opportunities to glean. It's amazing to discover how much abundance is growing in our communities when we take time to look. I often find a gift of a sunflower or an envelope of seeds is the very best gift of all.

Grow what you love and pass it on. — Emily

For my girls

For me, *Grow What You Love* is a gritty love letter. It exists because of all I've been given, the people who believe in me, my many successes and failures over the years, and the patches of earth here and there that I've had a chance to plant. For all of this and the book itself, I'm incredibly grateful. My thank-you list goes well beyond who's included here; however, here's my short list.

To my team at Firefly: Steve and Lionel for your thoughtful guidance and for entrusting me with this amazing project, and to all those working behind the scenes. To Marijke Friesen for your creative expertise, and a huge thank you to Sydney Loney, my editor and champion of all things beautiful. Jeff and Dori with West Cliff Creative and Clover Robin: thank you for helping make this book gorgeous.

None of this would have been possible without the support of my husband, Josh Murphy. Thank you for your vision, for putting up with my relentless love of growing things (another "kale something") and for not being afraid to tell me some of my bright ideas are simply terrible, while helping me hone the ones worth developing.

To my girls. Madison Kwasny, thank you for being an inspiration and cheerleader when I need it most. And Sinead Murphy, your kind nature and playful spirit help me see the world with fresh eyes.

To my mom, Maryann Hall. It's your trust in me that has led me to live life a little differently, but always with compassion. To my dad, Bob Perry, for passing along your love of nature. To my other parents, Leon Hall and Grace and Mark Murphy, thank you for your loving encouragement.

I'm also lucky to be surrounded by a remarkable community of people: Raleigh and Paul Conner — for everything; Kathryn Aalto and Julie Claussen, for your generous guidance; Maggie Shiels and Lawrence Donegan, it was you two who gave me the courage to start this project; Stephen Kent, for editing my early work; Michael Jager, for showing me what it is to be a creative wonder; Debbie Berne, for sharing your visual voice; and Elizabeth and Charlotte, for lending me your garden.

And of course, thank you to my grandmother, whose answer to everything in life was love.

UNITED STATES

HARDINESS AND EXTREME MINIMUM TEMPERATURE ZONES

The maps here will help you determine which plants may thrive in a particular location. The maps reference the lowest average annual winter temperature and are divided into 10-degree zones (see pages 16–17 for details). In the United States, this method of scale has been adopted by the USDA as the standard for determining hardiness zones. Canada takes a different approach to mapping hardiness zones; however, the Canadian government has created the map on page 265, which uses the USDA's extreme minimum temperature scale.

CANADA

Temperature (°C)	-56.7 to -51.1	-51.1 to -48.3	-48.3 to -45.6	-45.6 to -42.8	-42.8 to -40.0	-40.0 to -37.2	-37.2 to -34.4	-34.4 to -31.7	-31.7 to -28.9	-28.9 to -26.1	-26.1 to -23.3	-23.3 to -20.6	-20.6 to -17.8	-17.8 to -15.0	-15.0 to -12.2	-12.2 to -9.4	-9.4 to -6.7	-6.7 to -3.9	-3.9 to -1.1	-1.1 to 4.4	4.4 to 10	10 to 15.6	15.6 to 21.1
Zone	0a/b	1a	1b	2a	2b	3a	3b	4a	4b	5a	5b	6a	6b	7a	7b	8a	8b	9a	9b	10	11	12	
Temperature (°F)	-70.06 to -59.98	-59.98 to -54.94	-54.94 to -50.08	-50.08 to -45.04	-45.04 to -40.0	-40.0 to -34.96	-34.96 to -29.92	-29.92 to -25.06	-25.06 to -20.02	-20.02 to -14.98	-14.98 to -9.94	-9.94 to -5.08	-5.08 to -0.04	-0.04 to 5.0	5.0 to 10.04	10.04 to 15.08	15.08 to 19.94	19.94 to 24.98	24.98 to 30.02	30.02 to 39.92	39.92 to 50.0	50.0 to 60.08	60.08 to 69.98

CONVERSION TABLE

Inches/Centimeters
1 in. = 2.5 cm
6 in. = 15 cm
12 in. = 30 cm
18 in. = 46 cm

Feet/Meters
1 ft. = 0.3 m
3 ft./1 yard = 0.9 m

Teaspoons & Tablespoons/Milliliters
0.5 tsp. = 2.5 ml
1 tsp. = 5 ml
1 tbsp. = 15 ml

Cups/Milliliters
1/4 cup = 60 ml
1/3 cup = 80 ml
1/2 cup = 120 ml
1 cup = 240 ml

Pounds/Grams & Kilograms
1 lb. = 454 g
3 lb. = 1.4 kg
5 lb. = 2.3 kg

°F/°C
165°F = 74°C
170°F = 77°C
200°F = 93°C
300°F = 149°C
350°F = 177°C
375°F = 191°C
400°F = 204°C

ONLINE RESOURCES

Cornell University Home Gardening
www.gardening.cornell.edu/homegardening/index.html

National Garden Bureau
www.ngb.org

National Gardening Association
www.garden.org

SEED COMPANIES

Baker Creek Heirloom Seeds, Rare Seeds
www.rareseeds.com

Botanical Interests
www.botanicalinterests.com

Halifax Seed
halifaxseed.ca

High Mowing Organic Seeds
www.highmowingseeds.com

Johnny's Selected Seeds
www.johnnyseeds.com

Lake Valley Seed
www.lakevalleyseed.com

Renee's Garden
www.reneesgarden.com

Seed Savers
www.seedsavers.org

Territorial Seed Company
www.territorialseed.com

West Coast Seeds
www.westcoastseeds.com

ON MY SHELF

Find inspiration for growing in cookbooks, and look for a regional gardening guide specific to your area. The books I reach for most are either ones with recipes in them or *Golden Gate Gardening: The Complete Guide to Year-Round Food Gardening in the San Francisco Bay Area and Coastal California*, by Pam Peirce. However, here is a selected list of books from my shelf that you may find useful:

Four-Season Harvest: Organic Vegetables from Your Garden All Year Long, by Eliot Coleman

Groundbreaking Food Gardens: 73 Plans That Will Change the Way You Grow Your Garden, by Niki Jabbour

Raised Bed Revolution: Build It, Fill It, Plant It . . . Garden Anywhere!, by Tara Nolan

Growing Vegetables in Drought, Desert & Dry Times: The Complete Guide to Organic Gardening without Wasting Water, by Maureen Gilmer

My Pantry, by Alice Waters

Vegetable Literacy, by Deborah Madison

Petal, Leaf, Seed: Cooking with the Treasures of the Garden, by Lia Leendertz

The CSA Cookbook: No-Waste Recipes for Cooking Your Way through a Community Supported Agriculture Box, Farmers' Market, or Backyard Bounty, by Linda Ly

A NOTE ABOUT THE GARDENS

Because of a wonderful set of chance circumstances, I've found myself tending to several gardens at once.

The garden closest to home is my deck garden (see page 28). It's a hodgepodge container garden comprised mostly of troughs because they're light, durable and easy to move around. Greens, herbs, small fruit trees and strawberries grow remarkably well here.

Then, there's the garden I discovered while I was out trail running — I call it the Knoll (see above). It's a gorgeous set of two raised beds that weren't being used. I asked the owner if I could borrow the space and began planting there in spring of 2016. Crops are hit or miss because of summer fog, but most veggies flourish. The drip system and micro-spray heads I added make direct-sowing seeds a dream, and just a bike ride away from home, it's a place I always look forward to visiting.

What doesn't grow well in either the deck garden or the Knoll seems to thrive in my community garden plot — 31b (see pages 24–25). I'd been waiting for a plot for over two years, so when my name finally came up I couldn't say no — and I'm happy I didn't. There's something truly wonderful about sharing garden space with others, seeing what everyone else is growing and soaking in the borrowed views. If it weren't for the little voles that have taken up residence in my plot, all would be perfect.

INDEX

Italic page numbers refer to photos.